ALONG

THE

WAY

COLLECTED

ESSAYS, LETTERS AND REFLECTIONS

By

DONALD J. COLE

Executive Director

NO PARTIES AMERICA.ORG

Century International Publishing Company

Published by:

Century International Publishing Company

Houston, Texas, U.S.A.

Printed in the United States of America

ISBN 978-0-9679173-6-8

Table of Contents

THE COLLECTED LETTERS

REFLECTIONS   309

DEDICATION

IT IS THE DUTY OF NATIONS, As well as of men, to own up to their dependence upon the overruling power of God, and to recognize the sublime truth announced in the Holy Scriptures and proven by all history that, those Nations only, are blessed whose God is the Lord.

Abraham Lincoln

INTRODUCTION

When I made the decision to establish a National grass-roots advocacy organization to propose, promote and support across-the-board reform to restore America's lost values and tarnished image, my initial intent was to develop an organization plan and structure, identify specific areas of concern to be addressed, build and publish a website on the internet and start recruiting members, all across America.

As I got into the business of outlining the details of the organization, its mission and operational activities, I soon acknowledged the fact that there would be much re-thinking of numerous components of the initial overall plan. Early in the process, I made a decision to write a book that would serve as a guideline and roadmap for the organization.

I worked on developing details for the website and began work on the book manuscript. I also developed the format for the organization's Monthly Letter, which will be made available by subscription to the members. I wanted both the book and the Monthly Letter to be released in conjunction with the launch of the website.

As things moved forward, I became more and more conscious of a nagging little thought in the back of my mind that exploded into a question that demanded my full attention and an answer. I had the outline for the book completed; twenty-one chapters in three sections, and all of the Chapters started. I knew the launch of the NPA.Org Website was at least months away. There were many details to be worked, some of which were not yet even identified.

At some point in the process, I started thinking about the large body of work I had in hand, in the form of Essays, Letters and reflections I had written over many years that truly constitute the ideas and beliefs from a broad spectrum of issues and ideas that form a basis for the mission that NPA.Org will pursue; pieces related to National issues, Religious issues, Patriotism and political issues and events, upon which, NPA.Org will be formulated and organized.

I am a lifelong active, practicing Roman Catholic and, though not overly pious, seriously and sincerely committed to my devotion to my Lord and Savior. I remain, today, the soldier of Christ I became when I was confirmed at age eleven.

My writings clearly reflect the beliefs I hold: that our Nation and my beloved Church, the most important institutions in my life, both, face extraordinary threats and challenges from within and from outside their structures. As a Soldier of Christ and a Patriot, I stand in defense of these beloved institutions that are so dear and important, to me, my family, my friends and the world-at-large. With these thoughts in mind, I made the decision to compile this collection of my earlier works as a prelude to the launch of NPA.Org and my book, "The Party's Over", which will be released when the Website is officially launched.

I sometimes take positions in my writings that are uncomfortable to me, or even objectionable to National or Church leaders, or others in some way connected to the subject issue. I write what I believe in; truthfully and directly. I open up and hold nothing back. What I write is who and what I am.

Born in Brooklyn, New York, near the end of the great depression, the second of four siblings in a Catholic, American-Irish family, I am a second generation American. The elders of my extended American family; grandparents, parents, aunts, uncles, were all Democrats which, for various reasons, never attached to me.

As a youngster, growing up during the war years of WWII, seeing my uncles, cousins and many of our neighbors going off to war, I developed an early and uncommon (for a young child) sense of patriotism and duty. At the age of eight, I not only played "war" with my friends in the neighborhood, but avidly followed the war news reports in the papers, on radio, and in newsreels at our local movie theater.

For some reason I have never understood, I knew the importance of all that was going on in far off places around the world. I was six and a half years old when the Japs attacked Pearl Harbor on December 7, 1941 . . . six and a half years old. Yet I remember that day vividly. There was great commotion all over our neighborhood. Neighbors were out in the street and in and out of each other's homes, talking, discussing and arguing about what it all meant.

The common denominator; the thread that connected all of the discussion, was a compelling sense of importance and resolve, much like the unity we saw in the wake of the 9/11 Attacks. That was what registered in my young mind. It was the awakening of my own patriotism. It has never left me; never diminished in my mind and heart.

I love my country. I am, and always will be, enormously grateful for all of the blessings God has showered upon our beloved country. I am, unabashedly, a Nationalist.

In these days, where "globalism" and a "New World Order" are promoted by many as the new way of life, I hold fast to the fact that America, and only America, has been and remains, the sole bright beacon of freedom and justice for all the world to see and aspire to.

But my Country and my Church are under siege. I grieve for the lost innocence and the decaying moral values that are eating away at the vitals of our Nation – and, yes, My Church.

It is, for me, heartbreaking and infuriating to see the ever growing trivialization and disrespect for the traditions and values that made America so unique in the world.

I have identified a pattern that the enemies of America and our Judeo-Christian beliefs and values use in their war to destroy us. Pick any institution, tradition or widely held belief that is dear to our Nation or our Religious institutions – one that our enemies wish to destroy – and see if you recognize their four stage attack plan. First, they Trivialize the target Institution, Tradition or belief. Second, they Mock the target activity or institution. Third, they Demonize the target institution or belief. Fourth, they Criminalize the target. It is a very insidious process that has served their end very well for decades, as everyday Americans and Christians sleep.

The ingratitude of so many who pursue their own selfishness and greed, without a thought of the legions of America's finest men and women who gave all to purchase and secure our many freedoms – or any conscious concern for the perilous path to destruction we are following today, is extremely distressing.

I chose the entries in this book from the Essays and other writings I created over a period of many years, to reflect who I am and what I believe in.

I am well aware that I am just one person and lay claim to no prominence in the world. Yet, as ordinary a man as I am, I am convinced that there are many other ordinary men and women who, like me, care a great deal about preserving the American way of life and the Religious Freedoms endowed by it, passed down to us to preserve and protect.

For more than fifty-five years I was a loyal and active Republican, because the Republican Party best reflected and represented the conservative, traditional values I have always believed in – and still do. But, as anyone who recognizes the realities of present day politics in America can plainly see, it has become next to impossible to tell the Republicans from the Democrats.

Career politicians on both sides of the aisle are almost indistinguishable from one another. The underlying concern is that both Parties are occupied only with their own personal interests.

The interests of the Country; of the People these politicians are elected . . . *and paid* to serve, have no place on their agenda. Self-interest, greed and lust for power are the motivators for all but a small – and growing smaller – number of elected officials. We are in crisis. We need to reform and restore the luster to the American Dream; to that "Shining City On The Hill".

The "diversity" espoused by so many political and business leaders, is a scourge that is fracturing the

14

structure of our American way of life and rendering us more vulnerable to the enemies of freedom and American Values.

Where did this rhapsodic worship of so-called "diversity" come from? "UNITY" is what made America the greatest Nation in all of the history of the world. "Unity" is the desperately missing element in everyday American life today.

The "Diverse States of America" is an oxymoron. No clear thinking person with any understanding of the lessons of history could ever believe such utter nonsense.

Because I believe that the most important mission that we, who love America, have ahead is the Re-Unification of our United States, I made the decision to create a grass-roots organization committed to restoring our traditional values and freedoms.

Many of our Founders, Washington and Adams among them, were vigorously opposed to the "Party" System. In their wisdom, they saw the pitfalls of such a system. We see, today, the result they so clearly envisioned then. The Parties are terminally polarized; incapable of cooperating on even the most basic issues of the National Interest. Yet those same Parties, as clearly demonstrated by their actions, are virtually indistinguishable in their pursuit of Self Interest and unconcern for the people they are paid to represent.

Thus, this grass-roots organization, "No Parties America.Org" (NPA.Org) is dedicated to proposing, promoting and supporting across-the-board reform and restoration of traditional American values.

Just as the small band of American Colonists, who had a vision of freedom and justice, fought and overcame the mighty power and resources of the British Crown, the greatest power on earth at the time, and the fear and apathy of many of their own Colonist neighbors, to give birth to this great Nation, so, too, are those who join with us, committed to reclaiming and restoring our beloved Country.

Membership in NPA.Org is offered to any legally registered voter in all of the fifty United States. Members of the military and Ex-pat Americans working outside of the United States, who are legally registered U.S. Voters, may request membership through their home State's Division. There is no fee for annual membership. The free membership must be renewed annually, with verification of voter status.

NPA.Org is currently in the formation stage and will be organized as either a Corporation or a Limited Liability Company (LLC). The organizational structure consists of Administrative Officers, a Council of State Deputies and Assistant State Deputies and an Honorary Advisory Council. The Organization will not be organized as a Non-Profit. No tax deductible donation solicitations or any other any other solicitations for contributions to the organization will be made or accepted from the members or any other persons or organizations. NPA.Org will have no salaried employees. Administrative Officers, State Deputies, Assistant State Deputies and certain other operating managers will serve in their respective capacity with no salary. Various activities conducted by the organization, such as Reform Rallies, Patriotic Activities/Programs, Membership Drives and other events as become appropriate, may require an admission fee to cover costs of the events.. No NPA.Org Sponsored events will require mandatory attendance to maintain membership.

Membership in NPA.Org will be granted with the expressly stated expectation that members will, to the best of their ability, actively participate in the programs for which the organization exists; programs and activities that propose, promote and support restorative reform in a broad spectrum of American life, including, but not necessarily limited to:

- The Open Borders Threat to National Security
- Language Issues
- Disappearing American Culture
- The Growing Trade Deficit Bomb
- The Attack on Judeo-Christian Foundations
- The Specter of Islamo-Fascism
- Job Drain
- Election System Reform
- Term Limits

- Bureaucracy Reform
- Tax Reform
- Welfare reform
- Education Reform
- Military Reform
- Judicial Reform
- Immigration Reform
- Trade Reform

The terms and conditions for membership in NPA.Org are very simple and direct: Membership is offered to those qualified individuals who, having met the basic requirements for membership request membership with the express stipulation that such members will be active in NPA.Org business they are asked to participate in, to the fullest possible extent of their abilities.

The book you hold in your hand is a window into the enduring philosophy, upon which NPA.Org is founded and will follow in the pursuit of the organization's mission: To work diligently in the pursuit of the full recovery and restoration of the noble ideas of our Nation's Founders and the traditional values and moral fiber of our beloved Country.

My book, "The Party's Over" will serve as the guideline and roadmap for the day to day conduct of the organization's business to achieve the goal of full restoration of America's Leading place in the world. Consisting of three sections and twenty-one chapters,

"The Party's Over" will clearly define: The Problems. The Particulars, and The Solutions.

I invite and urge all who read this book and decide to join with us in this noble effort to raise our Nation back to her True Place as the brightest beacon of Freedom and justice in the entire world and to bring your families and friends with you on the journey. It will take all of us. And it will take time, resolution and determination.

WE CAN DO IT!

Donald J. Cole
Cypress, Texas   October 12, 2013

THE COLLECTED ESSAYS AND LETTERS

The Essays section of this collection contains Essays of varying lengths, presented in reverse chronological order covering the period from July 15, 2012 through June, 1998. The subject categories vary and the Essays are not grouped by subject category.

The Letters section of the collection contains sixteen letters and four reflections, also presented in reverse chronological order covering the period from June 15, 2010 through October 12, 1967. As is the case with the Essays, the subjects vary and are not grouped by subject category.

The Essays, Letters and Reflections are listed in the Table of Contents with a subject code in parenthesis. There are three subject category codes:

- Nation (N)
- Church (C)
- General (G)

An Essay, Letter or Reflection may be listed with a single code or, in some instances with two or all three codes when the subjects overlap or relate to more than one category. There are introductory comments preceding some of the Letters to provide background details and explain what precipitated the writing of the letters.

It is the Author's fervent wish that you will find something inspirational or challenging . . . or both, in each of these Essays and Letters. Their content is intended to provide a reflection of the life philosophy and commitment of the Author, and to inspire and promote your own ideas and reflections on the subjects presented.

COLLECTED
ESSAYS

236 Years And Counting The Grand Experiment Continues . . .

© Donald J. Cole, July 5, 2012

On Wednesday, July 4, 2012, we celebrated Independence Day, in observance of the 236th birthday of our Nation. I cannot recall a year when I was less enthusiastic about celebrating the occasion. I kept recalling the words of my old Navy Chaplain on the USS Yorktown during the Korean War, Father Ward. "God bless America" He would bellow . . . *"For What?"* Father Ward truly loved America with all his heart. His words were prompted by the fact that it broke his heart to see his sailors, when we were in port, carousing , drinking themselves into stupors and carrying on with prostitutes when he knew that so many of them had wives and girlfriends waiting for them at home. The good Chaplain's message resonated with me. Oh, I certainly was no saint; spent many a liberty getting drunk. But playing guitar and singing country music were my favorite activities in those days and that kept me clear of the nasty stuff.

As I reflected on the condition of our Country, the good Chaplain's words echoed loudly in my mind. I ask myself, **_Why, Indeed, should God bless Our Country_**? **_What have we done to deserve any further blessings from God?_** Could we have possibly asked or hoped for more blessings from God than he has so abundantly poured upon us?

The **Americans** who created this Country, 236 years ago, are long dead and buried. Who were those people? Where did they come from? What set them so much apart from the run of the mill? Where did they find the will? . . . the wisdom? . . . the resolve? . . . the courage? . . . and the decency? . . . to create the greatest, most noble government ever raised on the earth ?

The Decency! That quality, which set apart the American Experiment from anything ever seen before it, seems nowhere to be found in our present day lives; in our government; in our political parties; in some of our oldest institutions including, even, many of our Churches. What we see at the forefront of life in America today is **_Decay, Degeneracy_** . . . and a full, frontal assault on religious values and freedom; on our rights as American citizens to the absolutely unfettered pursuit of our religious beliefs, without any encroachment by the United States government or any of its subdivisions.

But, our government is desperately *out of control!* The **Executive Branch** is actively engaged in all manner of unconstitutional and illegal activity, **utterly unrestrained by the Congress**, The **Legislative Branch**, who stand idly by on the sidelines and refuse to perform their own sworn duty to the People, and who do little or nothing to restrain the **Rogue Executive Branch**. It is as though we are in Free Fall, with no one at the controls of the Ship of State as we hurtle toward utter destruction and oblivion.

I liken America's present course to that of the Mars Curiosity Rover Mission. Let me explain that comparison. The Landing in early August, 2012 of the Mars Curiosity Rover will be either a spectacular success or a devastating, massive failure. After journeying 345 million miles through space over eight and a half months, the actual Landing process (from the top of the Mars atmosphere to the Gale Crater landing surface) will take a mere *seven minutes* from start to finish and will involve several intricate, high speed maneuvers to safely complete.

Think about that for a moment . . . **Seven Minutes!**

And, if that is not incredible enough for you to comprehend, here's something else to wrap your brain around: the *Signal of the landing* will take *14 minutes to be received by Mission Control*. Thus, should the landing fail, the Rover will have already been dead on the surface of the Gale Crater for seven minutes . . . *as long as the entire landing process itself*, before we know the result. As I stated above, I see a parallel between America's present course and that of the Mars Curiosity Rover . . . it being the astonishing *uncertainty* of what will be the final result. That said, however, I hasten to point out that the Mars Mission Control Team has devoted years of research to discover every conceivable emergency that could develop in the course of the mission and to develop preventive and protective measures to deal with them.

Our Nation, by contrast, is rapidly traversing a course that our government has launched us headlong into, with *neither an identifiable destination nor a plan to reach it.*

I have faith in the Mars Curiosity Rover Mission due to the massive planning and sound scientific application of the best available technologies for success.

America's present course leaves me with nothing more than *a cold chill.*

It is almost more than I can process, to consider the differences between the Americans responsible for the creation of the Mars Rover Curiosity Mission and the *purported* "Americans" who are responsible for our nation's mindless plunge into the abyss that may spell our doom.

The recent Supreme Court Decision on the Obama-Care debacle serves to further illustrate the progressive decay of our Nation's corrupt ***Judicial Branch***. The Chief Justice of the United States Supreme Court, in his Written Decision for the Liberal majority on the Court, with whom he joined in the outrageous decision, producing a huge gag reflex in millions of True Americans .. a decision which is ***in conflict with the expressed wishes of 70% of Americans*** , stated . . . *"IT IS NOT OUR JOB TO PROTECT THE PEOPLE FROM THE CONSEQUENCES OF THEIR POLITICAL CHOICES."*

I would say to Justice Roberts: Really, Sir? Was Obama-Care the "Political Choice" of the PEOPLE, or NOT . . . as the public opinion and outcry against it emphatically show? And, *IF NOT*, then, why the unfortunate choice of words?

Was the learned Justice aiming for a "clever turn of phrase"? Here is just another breathtaking piece of evidence to show the devastation that has been wrought upon our American Values and Our Constitution.

With the enormity of the injury and damage being heaped upon us on a daily basis by the out of control renegade government, it would be more than reasonable to expect that *We The People* have had enough . . . have suffered all of the abuse and will suffer no more of it! It would be reasonable to assume that the Voters of this Nation would be raring to get to the

Polls and toss out all of the counterfeit and criminal elements in the government apparatus. ***But, are they?*** The 12 % turnout of registered voters in the recent Texas Republican Primary (that included a highly contested, mud-slinging, race for the seat of outgoing Senator Kay Bailey Hutchison), in my view, speaks volumes about my fellow Texas Republicans.

In my conversations with some of those folks, I've been told by some of them that there was no real need to vote in the Primary, because either one of the two main contestants (for the record: Lt. Gov. David Dewhurst and former Texas Solicitor General Ted Cruz) would be acceptable to them. Excuse me for saying it but, What Crap! What total garbage! Call it what you like . . . but I'll call it what it is: ***APATHY!***

If our beloved, once glorious, America dies . . . and it very well might . . . ***APATHY*** will be what ***KILLED*** it. And the people who embraced the APATHY will be the ***MURDERERS of AMERICA.***

Oh, to be sure, I can hear in my mind some of your protestations of outrage at such an inflammatory statement. I will leave those individuals to explain to their grandchildren (the ones that were not aborted for convenience sake) why they deserted their Country and their duty.

THIS IS A CALL TO AMERICANS WHO LOVE AND RESPECT OUR NATION AND ALL OF ITS FOUNDING

PRINCIPLES AND VALUES. THE CALL IS A CALL TO ACTION . . . A CALL TO GO TO THE POLLS ON ELECTION DAY AND DO YOUR DUTY TO YOUR COUNTRY. SHOULD WE FAIL IN THIS CALL TO DUTY AND LOSE OUR AMERICA, THERE WILL LIKELY BE ANOTHER CALL . . . LATER ON . . . LIKE THE CALL THAT THE AMERICAN COLONISTS ANSWERED WHEN THEY BUILT THIS NATION . . . AND WHICH CALL COST MANY OF THEM THEIR VERY LIVES TO BRING THE GREAT GIFT OF FREEDOM TO YOU AND YOURS.

PLEASE ANSWER THE CALL.

Hope Is The Mother Of All Men
Reflections on a Recollection

© Donald J. Cole   February 19, 2012

For much of my adult life, I have held an inspirational phrase in my mind that I have often pulled up from the far reaches of my consciousness, when faced with a particularly daunting situation that seemed to offer no satisfactory way through the crisis it presented. The Phrase has always lifted me up and resulted in my finding a way to resolve the crisis without any significant loss or injury. I believe most of us have a collection of those "go to" phrases in our minds that we pull into the front of our consciousness at those trying times that confront us with a challenge that may seem, at the time, to be more than we can handle. Everyone has heard one or more of those phrases and, probably, has drawn some strength from one on such an occasion. "When the going gets tough . . . the tough get going". You've heard that one, haven't you?

Or, how about, "God will never give you a burden that you cannot handle" (or words to that effect)? And, another of my personal standbys, "Never, Never, Never, EVER . . . give up".

The Phrase I write about here is shrouded in mystery for me. It is, simply: ***"Hope Is the Mother Of all Men"***. What makes it mysterious for me is the fact that I have a strong memory of having seen and heard the words for the first time, spoken by a character in a movie. My memory of seeing the words spoken on the screen is that the Actor, Montgomery Clift, spoke them in his role as Private Robert E. Lee (Prew) Prewitt in the film "From Here To Eternity". In the scene, Prewitt, who had been attacked and severely beaten, was speaking to his friend Maggio, played by Frank Sinatra.

I am more than a little puzzled by the fact that, as much as I have searched the on-line media; Google, etc., I have been unable to find any reference to the movie scene that I associate with the words of the phrase that has stayed with me for so many decades. It seems impossible to me that such a powerful phase could go un-noticed by those who immortalize such phrases from motion pictures. Perhaps my recollection of the source is incorrect. Yet my search for the source of the words has not turned up a scene from any other film.

This Essay is not about the movie, so I commend any further curiosity you may have about the film to a Google search. What I do wish to address in this Essay is the message and the power of the words of the subject phrase: "Hope Is the Mother of All Men". This past Sunday, we had a visiting Priest celebrating Mass at my Church. He introduced himself as Father Jose Maria, and said he was from Spain. In his Homily, he

31

referenced the three foundational virtues of Catholic teaching: Faith, Hope and Charity.

And, though the Church teaches that the "Greatest of these is Charity"; Father Jose stated that, for him in his life, Hope always has been his focus. Hearing his words triggered my memory of the words of the phrase that is the subject of this Essay.

I, too, believe that Charity is the greatest of the three virtues. Yet, I also believe that Hope may well be the most commonly sought by the largest number of people. The idea that "Hope" is the mother of all men resonates with me on a deep and personal level. I have carried that thought . . . that belief . . . in my heart and mind for all these many decades, and it has become a part of me. Many times, in the face of trouble, doubt and fear, I have called upon those words and drawn strength from them.

The whole idea of "Hope" in the face of uncertainty, danger and fear is surely one of the most powerful wells of wisdom, from which we humans draw the courage to act in challenging and threatening situations, a trusted source upon which we place our belief in God's power, care and mercy.

Regardless of the actual source of the words the Phrase is, for me, a part of my personal belief system. I truly believe in my heart and mind that "Hope *Is* the Mother of All Men".

SAFETY! 2 POINTS
. . . YOU LOSE

In Football . . . Two Points that can make you a winner . . . or a loser.

You saw it. On The Patriots first possession in the 2012 Super Bowl, Tom Brady, backed up to his own goal line tries to unload a desperate pass from his own end zone and gets nailed for a two point Safety. What a way to start a Super Bowl game!

As things turned out in the game, with New York winning the game by a score of 21-17, that two point safety was not the difference between winning and losing. Right? New York won by four points, not two.

That's true enough. But I would propose that giving up those two points in the Safety on their first possession of the game cost the Patriots more than two points. I don't know who made the call . . . probably Brady, but whoever was responsible, it cost a great deal more than two points. It never should have happened. But it did,

33

and the demoralizing effect on the team surely cost them more than the four points that were the winning margin.

The real damage was that the Safety at that early stage in the game caused the Patriots a serious loss of **concentration.** That was a major factor throughout the rest of the game.

That play brought back memories of a game I coached, many long years ago, that also involved a Safety, but ended very differently.

The Super Bowl Safety was itself the consequence of a **lapse in concentration.** The Safety in the long ago game that I am about to relate to you was a result of **not losing concentration**; that produced a very different and very satisfying result for the team that **"gave up"** the Safety.

I coached Youth Football for twelve years in Houston, Texas. I started out when I enrolled my two boys in F.U. N. (Football United National) Football in the early 1960's. F.U. N. Football was a league that consisted of teams from throughout the Houston Metro area.

Each Team paid a franchise fee to join the league. Each Team was administered by a Board and League rules were promulgated by the board. Fun Football was a very well organized program, with an excellent stadium that included a Press box with field phones for the opposing coaching staffs, an electronic Scoreboard and Home and Visitor locker rooms. There were four levels of competition: Junior Freshman (8-10 year olds), Freshman (8-10 year olds), Junior Varsity (11-12 year olds) and Varsity (11-12 year olds). The Freshman and Varsity Levels played for a League Championship. The Junior levels did not play for a Championship. But all played to win.

I chose to Coach on the junior Levels and went from the Junior Freshman to the Junior Varsity levels over approximately nine years.

The Junior level kids were the ones who did not have all of the natural ability. That's why I chose to Coach on the Junior levels. I wanted to help those youngsters develop their skills and abilities and especially to develop their confidence in themselves.

It was in a game between The Westbury Steers Junior Varsity (my team) and The West University Shamrocks Junior Varsity that a Safety was the difference between winning and losing . . . but not the way you might be thinking.

The Steers and the Shamrocks were arch-rivals, and both were good teams. In this game The Steers were leading late in the fourth quarter, 13-7, with 39 seconds left on the clock. We (the Steers) were on our own 3 yard line facing a fourth down. We did not have a punter . . . A very difficult situation.

I called time out and had my Tail Back (we ran a single wing offense and our tailback was the equivalent of our quarterback) come to the sideline. I instructed him to call a 46 (sweep right), take the snap and kneel down in the end zone. Bobby was a smart kid and looked at me as if I were crazy.

"Bobby", I said, "Don't think about it, just do it. Trust me." He did what I told him to do and I watched the other sideline, as they initially whooped and hollered and celebrated the Safety. Two points for the Shamrocks! Now it was 13-9 Steers. Then I watched as reality set in and gloomy looks replaced the smiling faces across the field.

Of course when you get a safety, you get a free kick from your own twenty yard line. Well, it so happened that the Steers did, indeed, have an excellent kick off kicker. We teed up the ball and the Shamrocks fielded the kick on their fifteen yard line. Our kick-off team was there with the ball and the play was downed on the nine yard line after the chase.

There were less than ten seconds on the clock. The Shamrocks last play got them up to their fourteen yard line.

GAME OVER!
Final score: Westbury 13 West University 9.

Who says a Safety is a bad thing? Well, that depends . . .

Advice From George Washington

© Donald J. Cole, February 4, 2012

IN COMMEMORATION OF THE 280TH ANNIVERSARY OF HIS BIRTH: THE FATHER OF OUR COUNTRY, HIS EXCELLENCY GEORGE WASHINGTON

On this dreary February Saturday morning, just eighteen days before the birthday of the man who is acknowledged to be The Father of Our Country, George Washington, I have just finished reading William M. Fowler Jr.'s excellent book, "American Crisis . . . George Washington and the Dangerous Two Years After Yorktown, 1781 – 1783". The book details the extraordinary difficulties that confronted our Commander-in-Chief during that dangerous period in the process of our Nation's birth.

If you are not familiar with the period, you really should be . . . we all should be completely familiar with the trials and the treachery of those early days that threatened the Nation's Army and its Commander-in-Chief, the Congress and America's struggle for Freedom and Justice.

I have studied the Revolutionary era and our Country's founders extensively and, It seems to me, every new book I read on the subject reveals new insights and facts that, along with information I was already aware of, convince me that such was the complexity and the depth of the creation of this Nation, I will likely never in my own lifetime learn all of the significant details.

As I read Mr. Fowler's book, though already well aware of Washington's legendary courage, character and deep faith in God, I marveled time after time at how amazing it was that the man was able to keep himself on course, keep his starving, struggling, unpaid army intact and avert the internal threats that might well have destroyed, forever, any hope of fulfillment of American Independence.

As the events chronicled in the book unfolded, I slowly became conscious of my own thoughts about comparisons of the perils Washington and our Nation faced during that period and the perils and dangers of destruction of American Independence we are facing in America today.

I believe very strongly . . . that no thinking, reasonably intelligent American, respectful of the truly glorious nature of American Independence and Freedom and the enormous courage, sacrifice and suffering endured by those Patriots who won . . . and who, once it was secured, have repeatedly preserved the great gift of Freedom they purchased for all of us living today . . . could fail to see the dangers that surround us *now*.

We are threatened by enemies throughout the world, which is not unfamiliar to us. We have always had external enemies. That is because evil always opposes good. Tyrants and Dictators and would be Tyrants or Dictators are the natural enemies of Freedom and Justice.

America has always faced and overcome the external threats to our existence and the peaceful extension of our hand to people in need of help all over the world. No other Nation . . . in the entire history of humankind . . . has ever come close or even approached coming close to the goodness and charity of America. But, today, we are faced with uniquely different circumstances that threaten the bedrock foundations of, not only our Nation, but our People, as well. The evidence is all around us, everywhere.

The Moral Fabric, the Faith, the Family, the Traditional American Founding Principles and Traditional Values . . . All . . . are under intense attack from many quarters, within our own borders, by citizens of our own Nation. We are a Nation in deep peril, on the threshold of Self-destruction. Look around you and see – *really see* – how desperately deranged our society has become.

We have so many breakdowns, on so many levels, of so many components of our overall society; it is a challenge to even make a list of our ills.

A renegade National Government Administration and Bureaucracy, trampling all over the United States Constitution and even *mocking* that sacred document; conducting criminal enterprises, refusing to perform the duties of their offices; a Judicial System in disarray; a Congress that does nothing to stop the bleeding and repair the damage; a failed educational system; attacks on religious freedom; an American Holocaust, sanctioned by the government, that has, since 1973, destroyed the lives of approximately fifty million babies; an Illegal Immigrant invasion that is bleeding us dry of employment, educational and health care resources, unchecked by our National government; the growing disintegration of the family and the accompanying abandonment of family values and responsibility.

My heart cries out to my Lord and Savior to descend upon our people and bestow His grace upon us to see the error and offense of our ways and turn back the tide of destruction that threatens to destroy our beloved Nation and all of us with it.

I wrote an essay in 1991 that began: "I can sum up what is wrong with America in three words: The American People."

That statement, regarded by some at the time as Cynical, was not cynical then. It was observant. The statement is truer today, by orders of magnitude, than it was then.

As critical as our National Condition is today, though, WE CAN Save America. WE MUST SAVE AMERICA. If America fails and sinks into the sea of failed Nations, the rest of the world will sink in our wake. Never before, in all of recorded history has so great a Nation, in terms of its size, its contributions to the advancement of humanity throughout the entire planet, faced the prospect of a total destruction of such magnitude . . . that would ultimately devastate the entirety of civilization.

WE, YOU and ME and US, are the ones who bear the responsibility to accomplish the rescue. The job is already underway. I am certain that you, every one of you who read these words, know very well and can see very clearly that we absolutely MUST have a tidal wave of change in our elected government in November 2012, and that that change, in turn, must establish a further tsunami of change in our entire Country to rescue and restore us.

I come now to the message of the Title of this essay, "Advice From George Washington" In the years 1781-1783, Washington, the Army, the Congress and the whole of our Nation weathered many crises that might well have been the death knell for America . . . not the least of which crises were created internally.

General Washington, Commander-in-Chief of the ailing American Army wrote: "A Circular Letter on the Distress of the Army Head-Quarters, Newburgh, New York, June 18 1783" [1] I offer you two excerpts from that letter that I pray will reinforce in you, the importance of the task at hand for all of us in 2012 to do everything each of us can do to save our beautiful Country, and inspire in you an understanding and appreciation for the blessings of such a rescue.

General Washington Wrote:

" . . . When we consider the magnitude of the prize we contended for, the doubtful nature of the contest, and the favourable manner in which it has terminated, we shall find the greatest possible reason for gratitude and rejoicing: This is the theme that will afford infinite delight to every benevolent and liberal mind, whether the event in contemplation be considered as the source of present enjoyment, or the parent of future happiness: and we shall have equal occasion to felicitate ourselves on the lot which Providence has assigned us, whether we view it a natural, a political, or moral point of light.

The citizens of America, placed in the most enviable condition, as the sole lords and proprietors of a vast tract of continent, comprehending all the various soils and climates of the world, and abounding with all the necessaries and conveniences of life, are now, by the late satisfactory pacification, acknowledged to be possessed of absolute freedom and independency; they are from this period to be considered as the actors on a most conspicuous theatre, which seems to be peculiarly designated by Providence for the display of human greatness and felicity: Here they are not only surrounded by everything that can contribute to the completion of private and domestic enjoyment, but Heaven has crowned all its other blessings by giving a surer opportunity for political happiness, than any other nation has ever been favored with.

Nothing can illustrate these observations more forcibly than a recollection of the happy conjuncture of times and circumstances, under which our Republic assumed its rank among the nations. The foundation of our empire was not laid in the gloomy age of ignorance and superstition, but at an epocha when the rights of mankind were better understood and more clearly defined, than at any former period" . . . "At this auspicious period the United States came into existence as a nation, and if their citizens should not be completely free and happy, the fault will be entirely their own."

"Such is our situation, and such are our prospects; but notwithstanding the cup of blessing is thus reached to us, notwithstanding happiness is ours, if we have a disposition to seize the occasion and make it our own; yet it appears to me, there is an option left to The United States of America, whether they will be respectable and prosperous, or contemptible and miserable as a nation: This is the time of their political probation; this is the moment, when the eyes of the whole world are turned upon them, this is the moment to establish their national character forever ."

" . . . It is only in our united character, as an empire, that our independence is acknowledged, that our power can be regarded, or our credit supported among foreign nations. The treaties of the European powers, with the United States of America, will have no validity on dissolution of the Union. We shall be left nearly in a state of nature, or we may find by our own unhappy experience, that there is a natural and necessary progression from the extreme of anarchy to the extreme of tyranny; and that arbitrary power is most easily established on the ruins of liberty abused to licentiousness."

IN CLOSING:

Please re-read that last Sentence . . . when I look

around me in America today, I am nearly overcome with sorrow and shame, at the sight of what surely looks to me like the beginnings of "the ruins of liberty abused to licentiousness".

I invite you to pray for our country, pray for our people, our families, our sacred and traditional American Institutions, our free, unfettered, peaceful and legitimate Religious Institutions, our Government and all of its divisions, agencies bureaus and departments, our judiciary, our courageous military and the Institutions to which they belong.

I invite you to pray for our enemies that they may hear the word of God and turn away from evil.I especially, I urge you to pray for the restoration of our National Character and for the courage, the wisdom and the determination to do your own part in accomplishing that restoration and make us, once again . . .truly . . . One Nation, Under God.

GOD BLESS YOU AND GOD BLESS AMERICA

NOTES:

1   The excerpts quoted are extracted from the Letter of June 18, 1782 found in Appendix 1, "AMERICAN CRISIS   GEORGE WASHINGTON and the Dangerous Two Years After Yorktown, 1781-1783"

Thoughts and Observations on Constitutional Government

While listening to a Talk Radio program a few days ago, the Host was interviewing his guest (both shall remain nameless here) and the phrase "Constitutional Government" popped up several times in the short conversation. As I reflected on those words, it occurred to me that those words are bandied about endlessly these days. It is almost impossible to see a day go by without the phrase "Constitutional Government" mentioned on radio, television or in print.

If I have my facts straight, "Constitutional Government" was born in these United States of America in the eighteenth century, after the American Colonies declared their independence from England and subsequently defeated the English in a deadly Revolutionary War for Independence. Our Founders created the United States' Constitution. The first "Constitution", known as the Articles of Confederation was approved by the Congress on November 15, 1777, during the course of the War. It was not until March 1781 that the Articles were ratified by all of the Thirteen Colonies.

Due to the weaknesses in the Articles of Confederation troubles ensued. George Washington and others made the case that the Articles were inadequate and in September 1786 delegates from five of the States met in Annapolis, MD and called for a full-scale meeting of all the states for "the express purpose of revising the Articles of Confederation". Congress approved and, on May 14, 1787, fifty-five delegates from all the states, except Rhode Island, met in the Philadelphia State House for the Constitutional Convention.

The delegates ignored any limitations to the business and purpose of the Convention, tossed aside the Articles of Confederation and created the draft for a completely new structure. Rhode Island's refusal to be part of the Constitutional Convention led the delegates to their decision to require only nine of the thirteen states to ratify the new Constitution to make it official. On June 21, 1788 New Hampshire quietly became the ninth state to ratify the Constitution. On November 21, 1789 North Carolina Ratified the Constitution that the new government was already operating under.

Rhode Island brought up the rear, two years after the Constitution had been officially ratified, voting ratification and becoming the last of the thirteen states to become a fully participating member of The United States of America on May 28, 1790.

The Bill of Rights and subsequent Amendments followed and our Nation has been and remains the greatest beacon and bastion of liberty and freedom in the history of civilization. Two hundred and thirty-five years have passed since the Declaration of Independence was signed by the courageous group of men whose faith in God and in themselves and the Nation they created produced the greatest document for guiding a Nation ever seen.

Obama . . . The Anti-Constitutional President

In the two years since Barack Obama took office and embarked on his Marxist path to engineer the destruction of America the astounding changes inflicted on America and Americans have brought this great Nation to the brink of complete destruction. We no longer have "**_Constitutional_** Government" in America! What the vile Obama Administration has wrought upon us is "**_Constipational_** Government" and it is slowly killing us. **_This government needs an enema! Now!_** We cannot continue to stand idly by, wringing our hands and whimpering about the sad state of affairs.

Last November, **_We The People_** sent the strongest message to Congress in decades that we have had enough!

We are fed up with the failure of Congress on both sides of the political aisle and we want decisive, strong action from them to stop the bleeding and get America back on the right course that our Founders strove and sacrificed so hard to produce and provide us with sound, principled guidance to make our great

Nation endure through the ages. Today, at this very moment, there are certain weak-kneed, perhaps *unprincipled* Senators and Congressmen wobbling and waffling on the serious changes that we the People want NOW.

Any of the Republicans in the House or Senate who fail to do their duty and do everything we sent them to do must . . . and surely will, be kicked out of office. We must have deep cuts in wasteful spending which must include repeal and defunding of the healthcare debacle and other programs . . . you know all the rest. Above all else, Obama's arrogant disrespect for the United States Constitution and the American People must be stopped immediately. He is a disgrace and an embarrassment to America and all that we stand for. It is long past time for articles of impeachment to be drafted and brought against this man on any number of a list of charges he should face, not the least of which is his violation of the oath of office in which he swore (or affirmed) defend and uphold the Constitution of The United States. We need a group of Congressmen and women to waste no more time; to have the courage and the principles to stand up and bring the charges against this Presidential impostor.

Call and write to your congressmen and women and your Senators and tell them in no uncertain terms that we are watching them, and we demand they do the job that we sent them to do or they will be replaced. PLEASE! Pass this along to as many people as you can. I repeat, PLEASE! Pass this along to as many people as you can, and ask them to join with us in this urgent struggle for our Nation's survival.

If you won't be part of the solution, that's your choice . . . and your right, under the Constitution. If you decide to make that choice, you might also want to start researching where you will go when America collapses into chaos and violence.

Words from the Father of our Country

The Father of our Country, George Washington's unfailing wisdom shines forth brilliantly in his Farewell Address:

". . . The basis of our political systems is the right of the people to make and to alter their Constitutions of Government. But the Constitution which at any time exists, till changed by an explicit and authentic act of the whole people, is sacredly obligatory upon all. The very idea of the power and the right of the people to establish government presupposes the duty of every individual to obey the established government. . . .

One method of assault may be to effect, in the forms of the Constitution, alterations, which will impair the energy of the system, and thus to undermine what cannot be directly overthrown. . . .

It is important, likewise, that habits of thinking in a free country should inspire caution, in those entrusted with its administration, to confine themselves within their respective constitutional spheres, avoiding in the exercise of one department to encroach upon another. The spirit of encroachment tends to consolidate the powers of all the departments in one, and thus to create, whatever form of government, a real despotism.
. . .

Of all the dispositions and habits, which lead to political prosperity, Religion and Morality are indispensible supports. In vain would that man claim the tribute of Patriotism, who should labor to subvert these firmest props of the duties of Men and Citizens. The mere Politician, equally with the pious man, ought to respect and cherish them. . . .

As a very important source of strength and security, cherish public credit. One method of preserving it is, to use it as sparingly as possible; avoiding occasions of expense by cultivating peace, but remembering also that timely disbursements to prepare for danger frequently prevent much greater disbursements to repel it; avoiding likewise the accumulation of debt, not only by shunning occasions of expense, but by vigorous exertions in time of peace to discharge the debts, which unavoidable wars may have occasioned, not ungenerously throwing upon posterity the [burden], which we ourselves ought to bear. The execution of these maxims belongs to your representatives, but it is necessary that public opinion should cooperate. . . .

In offering to you, my Countrymen, these counsels of an old and affectionate friend, I dare not hope they will make the strong and lasting impression I could wish . . .

I have been guided by the principles which have been delineated. The public records and other evidence of my conduct must witness to you and to the world. To myself, the assurance of my own conscience is, that I have at least believed myself to be guided by them. I am unconscious of intentional error, I am nevertheless to sensible of my defects not to think it probable that I may have committed many errors. Whatever they may be, I fervently beseech the Almighty to avert or mitigate the evils to which they may tend. I shall also carry with me the hope, that my Country will never cease to view them with indulgence; and that, after forty years of my life dedicated to its service with an upright zeal, the faults of incompetent abilities will be consigned to oblivion, as myself must soon be to the mansions of rest."

The Cancers . . .
Destroying America From
Within . . .
An Update . . . One Year later

Donald J. Cole, April 7, 2010

Donald J. Cole, March 8, 2011

Cypress, Texas

There are many types and variations of Cancers that invade the human body. Left untreated most cancers, perhaps all cancers, can ultimately cause the physical death of the patient. I am not an oncologist, but a layman, seasoned by living on this planet, in this Beautiful and Noble Country for three-quarters of a century, and richly blessed with at least a serviceable body of knowledge about the cycles of life of Creatures and   Institutions.

I have made no attempt to quantify and catalogue the number of Cancers that invade the human body.

The Webster's American English Dictionary provides two definitions for the noun *Cancer*. 1: malignant tumor that tends to spread. 2: slowly destructive evil. Two definitions for the adjective *Malignant* are also provided. 1: harmful. 2: likely to cause death. Armed with the knowledge contained in these two definitions, any normal, thinking person can readily understand the extremely important and serious nature of those two words. I am not writing to address the first definition of

Cancer. The focus of this essay is on that second definition of Cancer . . . *Slowly Destructive Evil*, and on both definitions of Malignant, as they apply to our Beloved Nation.

As decent people, we have a moral obligation to offer aid and assistance, according to our own means and ability, to a family member, friend, or any human being to secure appropriate treatment when a tumor attacks that person's body, with the intent of saving and preserving that human life and restoring the person to good health. We are exhorted in scripture to be our brothers' keeper. We are directed to:

- Receive one another
- Edify one another
- Serve one another
- Bear one another's burdens
- Forgive one another
- Submit to one another
- Exhort one another
- Consider one another
- Be hospitable to one another

Our individual moral obligations extend beyond being our brother's keeper. By extension, we are obligated to protect and preserve the gifts and blessings we have received from God. In America, not the least of God's Gifts to us is this great nation, founded in His Holy Name to be the beacon of freedom and justice for all earth. At this moment, in April, 2010, we Americans have failed, collectively, to honor our moral obligation to preserve God's gift of this glorious nation . . . that our founders and generation after generation who followed them did, indeed preserve, millions of whom

54

sacrificed their own lives to preserve God's wonderful gift to all of us who share in it this very day.

No longer a Nation United in the common endeavors of Freedom, Justice and Truth, we are divided and distracted; no longer united in the common goals our forefathers, who struggled and suffered to establish the many blessings their struggles, Suffering and sacrifice have given to us. As a Nation; as a People; we are sick! Consequently, our weakness; our sickness; our collective lack of courage and responsibility, have brought about a potentially lethal attack on America by a host of Cancers that threaten, *if not treated and cured*, to cause the death of our wonderful country.

Yes, I stand to say to all who will hear me: our country has been invaded by numerous cancers. These cancers have been inflicted on America by us, The American People! We are the Cancers! Study the partial list of cancers below and search your soul to determine if you are a "carrier" of any of them:

Avarice	Communism	Socialism
Immorality	Cowardice	Greed
Treachery	Marxism	Narcissism
Relativism	Selfishness	Secularism
	Racism	

In creating the above list, my first idea was to try to list the cancers in some sort of ranking. That was more than what I thought appropriate. I believe each of us will have our own idea of what the ranking is or should

55

be from most dangerous to least dangerous. The list above does not qualify as an exhaustive summary of all of the cancers spreading through our nation. There are more. I chose those above because I believe most, if not all of the others not listed here could be considered a strain of one or more of those that are listed.

Our Nation is sick and needs us . . . all of us . . . to come to her aid; to make every effort, sacrifice anything we must to save her. No one can save America but us . . . The American People. The task is no small one. Nor, will the task be accomplished if we are not willing to suffer and sacrifice in order to heal our beleaguered land and restore it to good health. The first, most important, step in the process is simple. We must rise up against the powers that have driven God out of our day to day lives and our Nation's institutions . . . and RESTORE GOD'S CONSTANT PRESENCE in our daily existence.

There are many in America today, masquerading as "Americans", who do not love this country or our people, who through their monumental ignorance and arrogance deny God's existence, and who would not; will not, lift a finger to help our nation. That is because they are toxic components of the deadly cancers spreading through America's vitals. They are not Americans! They are our enemies. Make no mistake about that. To those vermin, I caution: persist in your degradation of our country and you will ultimately be revealed for what you are, and dealt with accordingly.

It is important to understand the methods these enemies of America employ to do their dirty work. There are four fundamental stages or phases they use to attack and destroy America's treasured ideals and institutions, including our various religious convictions and institutions:

- Stage One
  Trivialization
- Stage Two
  Mocking/Ridicule
- Stage Three
  Demonization/Criminalization
- Stage Four
  Banning and/or Outlawing

The four stages are employed in any kind of circumstance, directed at any individual, organization, institution, traditional practice, or observance. It is a remarkably simple process, as most evil enterprises are. One example of the process, in action, is prominent in the current news. I refer to the issue of the U. S. Military's so-called "Don't Ask, Don't Tell" (DADT) policy. The policy is currently the target of an intense attack by the "Gay, Lesbian, Bisexual, Transgender" (GLBT) bunch. In fact, Secretary of Defense Robert Gates, caving in to the Gays' attack on the policy, recently announced changes – relaxations to DADT.

This is an issue that turns most people off. But allow me to cut to the chase.

Gay activists have, for many years, been attacking organizations and institutions in an effort to elevate their deviant lifestyle to that of just another of any number of alternative lifestyles that are equally acceptable in society. The so-called "Gay" lifestyle is NOT an acceptable alternative in the eyes, and in the minds, of Christians and people of numerous religions who respect God's word.

The term "Gay" being applied to the homosexual lifestyle is, in itself, an indication of the delusional aspect of the minds of these deviant individuals. The homosexual people I know and have known throughout my long life are and have been overwhelmingly troubled, depressed and essentially anything but "gay", in the true sense of the word. Yet they use the word, in their attempt to portray their deviant lifestyle in a light and positive way. They delude themselves with the contrived notion that all is well when, in fact, the homosexual lifestyle is not "gay", but is really a dreary and desperately sad way to live the life God has given to them.

There is no intent here to analyze the origins and causes of what makes one a homosexual. There is, indeed, a vast lack of valid information concerning what makes a homosexual. It is my own deeply held belief that the field of Medicine, throughout time and history has failed to study the issue adequately and find answers that would possibly relieve the societal pressures of the issue.

I do not hate "Gays", however much I despise their deviant attempts to pervert reality and destroy the sacred institution of the sacrament of Holy Matrimony. *Nor is the focus of this essay a discussion or analysis of homosexuality.*

THE EXAMPLE OF THE CURRENT BATTLE CONCERNING "DADT" IS INCLUDED HERE TO *CLEARLY AND EMPHATICALLY* ILLUSTRATE HOW OUR ENEMIES EMPLOY THE FOUR STAGES TO ATTACK AMERICA AND AMERICANS

Openly declared, practicing homosexuals do not belong in the United States Military. Period. Our enemies will do anything they can to weaken or destroy our military preparedness. We must not allow that to happen.

The real issue under discussion here is simply that the GLBT Activist organizations (Which, by the way, I do not believe represent all homosexuals) have persisted in their twisted efforts to destroy American traditional values with the four stage plan. They have long publicly trivialized the normal and natural beliefs of Americans that homosexuality is unnatural. They have long mocked decent Americans who hold such beliefs. They are well advanced in the third stage of demonizing, and even to some extent, *criminalizing* natural behavior that conflicts with their twisted and perverted beliefs. And in many parts of our country they are well on the way toward banning or outlawing Americans from believing and practicing God's Law

Barak Obama has stated that he will "repeal the law that denies gay Americans the right to serve". God Forbid! If Obama succeeds in the pledge, it will be the beginning of the ruination of our great military.

There you have an example of how our enemies (and, yes, I consider the GLBT Fascists to be our enemies) use the four stage process in their war on us and on our country.

To those who are not "masquerading" as Americans but have simply become soft and lazy, or greedy and self absorbed, I say **Wake Yourselves Up**. Look into the mirror of your soul. Confront your failures and shortcomings; the behaviors that have contributed to our Country's illness. Be truthful to yourself and brutally honest in your self assessment. Acknowledge anything in yourself that must be fixed, and Fix It! Then:

STAND UP AND FIGHT!

The battle is raging on many fronts. Pick the one that is closest to your heart and get into the fight. Turn off your TV. Put it into mothballs for the duration. Get yourself to meetings and rallies. Bring your families and friends. Never, never, never, ever, give up or give in to the notion that this fight is too big for you. IT IS NOT! Organize groups of friends and family, colleagues and associates at work, fellow church members. Conduct meetings and develop plans to deal comprehensively with your chosen task. Network with other individuals and groups engaged in your task or any other of the many tasks to be accomplished. Scrutinize every issue and event that poses a potential threat to America on any front. Meet every such threat with an equal and opposite action.

Are You Getting This?

The Free Ride into decadence and, ultimately, to destruction is over. You MUST join in this struggle. You MUST carry your share of the load. You MUST make every contribution or sacrifice necessary. You MUST find the courage to carry the day. OR . . . *you will die with the Nation.* Picture, in your mind, what would happen to you, your family, your friends . . . if America is destroyed? How would you explain to your children or grandchildren why you did not stop those things that destroyed their homeland? How would you live? Where would you go to find a better life? If America is destroyed, the entire world will sink into the abyss, in her wake.

It Is Time For A Gut Check!

You hear a lot of talk these days about "Tea Parties". If you pay attention to the misinformation in the "mainstream media" (How's that for an Oxymoron? The media is far enough removed from mainstream Americans as to be on another planet) they would have you believe that Tea Parties are a huge Right Wing

Organization, massed to create disruption to the well oiled left wing collection of misfits, perverts and thieves that comprise the current government administration and its supporting apparatus.

The reality is that the "Tea Party" phenomenon is not a single organization but, rather, an undetermined number of groups of like minded people; Patriots committed to the restoration of America's Founding Principles. These groups consist of individuals who love this country and are dedicated to getting rid of the cancers that are eating away at the vitals of America.

The left wing misfits and perverts that make up the Obama Administration cannot comprehend the Tea Party concept, because it does not fit with the herd mentality of the leftist haters of our American way of life . . . which they want to destroy.

Nor, do the leftist frauds who occupy the current administration believe that their days are numbered. These enemies in our midst believe they are invincible. They have awakened Americans from sea to sea and border to border to the nature and extent of the threat to our National survival that they represent. They must be defeated. *With your help*, they will be defeated.

To meet and extinguish the threat, we must unite as American Patriots to expose and defeat these America hating frauds. It is a challenge of monumental proportions that will require all of the courage and determination you can muster. Are you ready for this fight? *Will you* join and give your best efforts to the cause of American Freedom and virtues?

Remember that time waits for no man. If you, that is *YOU*, the individual who is reading this, will not gather the strength and the courage to join this fight for the survival of our beloved country and our treasured way of life, then go on your way and do not seek salvation from those who will carry on the fight, when you find your freedom and security gone . . . lost in the vapors of the deceitful lies of those who are the cancers that seek our destruction. Go away from our midst, for you will not be welcome in our company after the battle is won. You will have no place in our society . . . nor will you deserve such a place, due to your cowardice.

Stand Up And Fight! Join The Battle To Reclaim Our American Heritage And Way Of Life!

My fellow Americans, Brothers and Sisters, all, there is no time to waste. The enemy is inside the gates. We are besieged from all sides . . . from within and outside our borders. We are in a desperate state of peril and our very survival, as the world's greatest hope is in grave danger. So what are you made of? Can you compare yourself to the Colonists of early America? Can you match their devotion and dedication to this glorious thing that is AMERICA? If so, then get moving . . . NOW . . . Today!

Learn More . . . For additional information about how you can join the effort, and make a difference in the cause to reclaim and rebuild Our America, send email to: tgst@att.net. Subject: America.

The Three "C's"
For Living a Catholic Soldier
of Christ's Life

Δ Contemplation Δ Commitment Δ Courage
I became a Soldier of Christ in 1946, when I received the Sacrament of Confirmation at St. Thomas Aquinas Church in the Diocese of Brooklyn, New York and added my Confirmation name, Aloysius, to my middle name, Joseph. I chose the name of St. Aloysius because I had learned he was the patron saint of purity and I aspired to always have a pure heart. God will one day judge the degree of the success of that aspiration.

On that day, when the Bishop gave me the, then customary, slap on the cheek and announced: "You are now a Soldier of Christ", it was truly a transformative experience. Those words pierced my consciousness as no other words ever had. It was as though I had been lifted up above the assembly and touched by the hand of God. From that day to this moment, the power of those words remains firmly in my mind and my heart.

I remain that Soldier of Christ.

In these troubled times, throughout the world, danger of epic dimensions never seen in history, threatens to destroy much of humanity. Warnings abound that we must make course corrections to avoid complete destruction of the world as we have known it.

This essay is intended to sound a call to those who desire to ward off the catastrophic consequences of doing nothing to correct our course and save all that is good in God's eyes. It is for you to decide your own place in response to what is presented here.

Contemplation

Being a Soldier of Christ does not make one's life easier. The predominant attitudes and opinions in the present day Catholic Church that I observe in my daily life appear to mostly reject, even mock, the very concept of anyone being a Soldier of Christ at all, which I consider to be just one more of the manifestations of the quiet cancer that is slowly killing the Catholic Church . . . along with the rest of the Christian Churches in America and the Western world in general. I believe the Catholic Church in Italy, for example, is as sick as the Church in America; perhaps even sicker.

It is not fashionable to declare one's self to be a Soldier of Christ. The touchy-feely Utopians that appear to constitute the majority or very near majority of Catholics today feel uncomfortable and threatened by words like Soldier of Christ in much the same way as they are uncomfortable and even repulsed by the characterization of the Mass as: the *Holy Sacrifice* of the Mass, or the *Un-bloody reenactment* of the *Sacrifice of Calvary.*

Such words and concepts evoke fear in the hearts of these Utopian Usurpers of Jesus Christ's Holy Catholic Church. Am I saying, then, that these people I characterize as Utopian Usurpers are evil agents of Satan? Perhaps some of them are, indeed, consciously engaged in the work of Satan. If so, I believe they would be a small number.

The majority of these Utopians, who have so damaged the health of the Church, that I am hearing statistics stating that as much as sixty percent of baptized Catholics in America . . . *sixty percent . . .* no longer attend Catholic Mass or no longer belong to the Catholic Church. The actual percentage may be smaller . . . or larger, by some small margin of error that would not significantly alter the condition of the Church that the statistical data reveals.

Our Church is in danger. The danger has been growing inside the Church for at least four decades employing the *perpetual growth* philosophy of Cancer . . . and the cancer continues to grow even today.

The news is not all bad, though. There are encouraging signs appearing in our midst. The true Catholics in the

Church are awakening to the crisis of the damage that has been inflicted on our beloved Church over the past forty years. We who embrace the teachings of the Church have been taught since early childhood to be obedient. Now we are awakening to the realization that we have been obedient to a fault; have been blindly obedient and have failed to observe and react to the many warning signs that the Church was under attack and was in the process of being deconstructed under our very eyes.

Our commitment to be obedient obscured our observations and subdued the instincts to act to reverse the damage and save the Church.

But the Church will, indeed, be saved. Neither Satan's agents, nor hoards of enemies of Christ and His Church, nor millions of misguided, delusional utopian believers, will ever succeed in destroying the Holy Catholic Church. The task of restoring the Church will be long and arduous, requiring great efforts and great sacrifices. We will be severely tested in the process. We will need many millions of Soldiers of Christ to confront and overcome the many known and, at this point, unknown challenges . . . pockets of cancerous growths within the body of the Church that will have to be repaired or removed.

We need Priests and Religious . . . *Real* Priests; *Strong, Manly, Courageous* men . . . not feminized, namby-pamby, sissified utopians without even one foot in the real world.

We need *Real* Religious Brothers who, though they do not feel a call to the Priesthood, are called to *serve God* in Religious life.

We need *Real* Religious Nuns who want to serve God . . . not as emancipated Feminist activists, but as Women, *consecrated to His service* in nurturing roles, such as teachers, nurses, etc.; not in competing traditional Men's roles, but traditional supportive roles, as we see in the Biblical characterizations of the roles of Women as they differ from the Biblical characterizations of traditional Men's roles in life.

The parallel threats and injuries of: Vatican Council II, The Sexual Revolution, The Drug Culture, The Anti-War Movement, and The Feminist Movement.

Vatican Council II

The Second Vatican Council was heralded as a great milestone in the history of the Church. The notion was that the Church was *too closed off to the world-at-large*, that we needed to open the windows of the Church and let in fresh air to rejuvenate the Church and reap all of the imagined benefits that would follow the great opening of the Church.

I wondered at the time who had determined that the Church was too closed off to the rest of the world (a statement I heard over and over, ad-nauseum). I wondered, too, what was meant by the notion of *opening the windows of the Church* and what the mystical, magical rejuvenation was to be gained, and from what source, or sources? Underneath all of the mumbo-jumbo, I feared, there was an injection of *secular humanism* and an embracing of some of the more tantalizing pleasures of the world outside the stuffy and repressive Catholic Church. Could it *be*? It could . . . and it was . . . and continues to be . . . and must be reversed.

I propose to you that the revolution, the culture and the two movements mentioned in the sub-title above have all played, and continue to play, a part in the de-construction of our Church.

Please allow me to explain my analysis. Then, if you share my view, join me, as a Soldier of Christ, and join the battle to rid the Church of the elements that are destroying over two thousand years of Catholic tradition.

Just prior to the Second Vatican Council, there were a number of Catholic Bishops, mostly in Europe, who were on the verge of being excommunicated from the

69

Church for their heretical views and actions that were in direct and open conflict with the Church. When the Council convened, those Bishops managed to not only avoid excommunication, but actually succeeded in gaining positions of power in the "new" Church.

The Sexual Revolution

The so-called Sexual Revolution was perceived to be the product of radical college students, generally acknowledged to have been launched in 1965. The so-called Sexual Revolution was actually the product of left wing radicals who were known as "Hippies" and "Flower Children", whose influence quickly spread to many College campuses throughout the nation. The "Free Love" movement recruited huge numbers of college students and young adults (though the word *adults* barely attaches to those reckless and tawdry individuals who embraced the concept).

Nothing good can be said of the so-called Sexual Revolution. Nothing! The most notable product of it was an epidemic of sexually transmitted disease (STD's) and the behaviors that led to the emergence of the era of Human Immune Deficiency (HIV) and AIDS, which has resulted in the deaths of hundreds of thousands of people around the globe.

Yet the Sexual Freedom mindset persists to this day. Sexual irresponsibility and sexual perversion have exploded in the general society and show no signs of diminishing. The practitioners of this "sexual freedom" lifestyle totally reject any semblance of religious values or principles. The hedonistic advocates and devotees of the free love movement have no room in their lives for God or Religion.

The Drug Culture

The Drug Culture grew out of the free love mindset of the so-called Sexual Revolution and has brought pain and misery to tens (perhaps hundreds) of millions of Americans and others around the world. The drug culture is worse than ever today and is the main cause of criminal activity that threatens to destroy nations if it is not reversed. The Drug Culture is an insidious threat to the world and growing worse with each passing year.

It is generally acknowledged that the Illicit Drug Industry is a multi-billion dollar annual industry in America. In light of that, it follows, naturally, that literally millions of Americans are *clients* of that industry. These are people from all walks of life, from top to bottom. Consider, if you will, the religious convictions or commitment of those millions of Americans.

The Anti-War Movement

The so-called Anti-War Movement emerged at about the same time as the so-called Sexual Revolution, in the 1960's, during the Viet Nam War. It was a creation of radical left-wing organizations; Socialists, Communists and assorted other anti American groups.

The people involved in the vanguard of the so-called Anti-War movement were also very much Anti-Catholic, generally Anti-Religion and, yes, Anti-American.

The Feminist Movement

Then, of course, we come to the so-called "Feminist" movement. This movement could more accurately be called The Lesbian Movement, or The Man Hatred Movement, or The family Hatred Movement. This "movement" was created under the guise of seeking "equal rights" for women, but has never been about equal rights for women. From its beginning, The Feminist Movement, or The Women's Movement, as it has also been called, has never been about equal rights for women. The leaders of the movement have been and continue to be radical Lesbian activists whose primary aim is to emasculate men and undermine the institution of the Family, and Family values. They have made great progress toward their goal. Millions of American men today have been emasculated and feminized to the extent that they are no longer capable of fulfilling the traditional role of a man.

That development has, in turn, created an upsurge in homosexual activity and activism as well as a parallel surge in Lesbian activism. Who among us with eyes to see and ears to hear cannot be aware of the radical movements to establish homosexual and Lesbian lifestyles as just another perfectly acceptable and normal, alternative lifestyle? Simply another way to live . . . What's more, these sexual deviants want to teach, and have succeeded in some places in teaching our school children that their perverted lifestyles are just as valid and normal as the natural heterosexual lifestyle that   God   created.

Where are the leaders of the Church?
Through all of the turmoil and perversion referenced above, The Bishops, who are supposed to be the vanguard, the Guardians of the Church have, for the

most part, been either detached from the attacks on our faith and beliefs or, even worse, complicit in the degradation that has so terribly devastated our beloved Church.

Our Bishops, with *very few notable exceptions*, are adrift, going along to get along, to the detriment of our beloved Church.

Far too many of our Bishops have grown accustomed to the luxurious lifestyle most of them enjoy, with constant pampering by bloated staffs that tend to their every whim.

All the while, these Bishops, with few exceptions raise no voice and take no action to address, on any meaningful level, the perversion so rampant in much of our society, turning a blind eye to the celebrities and prominent political figures who present themselves to the general public as Catholics and openly thumb their noses at Catholic teaching and live their lives in direct conflict with Catholic teaching and tradition.

Why do the Bishops, Princes of the Church, stand, no, *sit* idly by and do nothing to restore Catholic virtue and teaching in the Church? I propose to you that many of the Bishops have grown soft and self-absorbed in their plush lifestyles and are nothing more than modern day Pharisees. These men . . . and they are, after all, just men, must be confronted and informed that they are not performing their sacred duties to protect the Church and Lead their flocks.

Most Catholics I know would shrink from the idea of confronting a Bishop and expressing their belief (even though it is, in fact, their belief) that the Bishop is derelict in his duties. Why is that? The time has long since come when the Church Laity . . . the Faithful . . . who, as the Church teaches, in fact, **are the Church**, must stand up in defense of the Church. It is our duty, yours and mine, to defend the Teachings of the Church and protect the Church from her enemies, evil or otherwise, who would destroy her.

The parallels between Our Church and Our Nation

Any person possessed of reasonable intelligence should have no difficulty seeing the many parallels between the crises in our Church and the crises in our Nation,

The decay we see in the traditions and teachings in the Church are mirrored by the matching decay and perversion we see all around us in our everyday lives. One need only to monitor the typical fare on TV, visit a local Shopping mall or scan the typical content of the so-called social media on the internet for a single day, to get an accurate assessment of just how far down the slippery slope to destruction we have come as a People. What happened to America? What happened to our Church (and many other Churches as well)?

Cancer does not STOP (passive). Rather, Cancer must be STOPPED (active). That means, quite simply, that we . . .you and I . . . must take the action to STOP the destruction of both our Country and our Church.

Contemplation leads to Commitment . . .

Commitment

It is widely acknowledged that Americans are generally a friendly and easy going people. We are interested in life and generous to those in the world around us. We care. We also tend towards maintaining the Status Quo. We don't like to rock the boat or change horses mid-stream. We are a peaceful people.

When we are attacked, though, taken advantage of for our kindness and generosity; when we suffer injury from people who hate us . . . we are capable of a ferocious, astonishing response to evil.

In December 1941, Japan, in its evil attempt to conquer and rule the world, chose to conduct a sneak attack on the United States at our Pearl Harbor Naval base in Hawaii, massively damaging our fleet and aircraft and killing thousands. The attack severely crippled our defensive capabilities. Americans woke up to that devastating attack on a quiet Sunday morning and recognized the savagery of the Japanese and their evil ambitions.

Americans united in the war effort and saved our Nation and, quite frankly, the rest of the free world as well. Japan endured absolute and utter defeat, disgrace and humiliation as a result of the evil they brought upon the earth. And yet, in the aftermath, America, the greatest, most caring and generous Nation on earth, rebuilt Japan and restored their country to a condition better than it had ever been.

Yet again, in the 1980's Japan sought to conquer America, not militarily, but economically, as if to prove the fact the evil always exists in the world as the enemy of all that is good in God's creation. Japan's economy collapsed and remains in distress on this day in February 2011.

I view American Christians as what might be considered "Hybrid" Christians. I base my view on the unique end result of the combination of Christianity and America's Christian based foundational virtues, values and principles. I believe being a Patriotic American steeped in and embracing of the pure goodness of America's focus, from the early days of our founding to the present, on freedom, fairness and friendship, reinforces our personal commitment to true Christian Values and beliefs. That is not to say that *every* American fits the description presented here.

Clearly, there are many in America who do not share and embrace the values and beliefs described above. There are many Christians, both here and throughout the world, who do not accept, embrace or practice the virtues and teachings of Christianity, though many of those same individuals (including those in governments) present themselves as and proclaim themselves to be devout practitioners of the Christian faith . . . all while advocating, endorsing and practicing behaviors and beliefs, such as the killing of unborn or partially born children . . . an American Holocaust of astounding proportions, wrought upon us, against the will of the American People.

These enemies of Christian and American virtues and beliefs are diametrically opposed to the teachings of Jesus Christ and His Church. They have infiltrated our government and must be exposed, rooted out and punished for the damage they have caused to this great Nation. Such individuals, regardless of whether or not they hold powerful government positions, are *exceptions.* They do not represent the whole of Christian or American Virtues and Teaching. Those individuals will one day have the opportunity to give an accounting of their lives to the God of us all, Who alone, will evaluate and judge them.

I discuss "exceptions" here for two reasons. First. It is correctly known that there are exceptions to every rule. That is a time tested truth. We learn of it from early childhood and see/experience repeated manifestations of the validity of the truth of it. Second. As human beings . . . all created by, and in the image of the same one God . . . we are, nevertheless, not perfect. We are exhorted to strive toward perfection and to imitate the perfection of God in order to become as close to perfection as we can be.

Recognizing our own imperfections and acknowledging that we must work to overcome such flaws as we may have, presents an opportunity to us to mend our ways and *commit* ourselves to a higher standard of purpose and performance.

Committing one's self to being a "Soldier of Christ" means embracing the duty and responsibilities of the position across the entire platform of one's life; both the religious and the secular aspects of that life. The religious and spiritual duties and the Patriotic duties are intertwined into one bond. We live no portion of our lives in a vacuum. For that reason, there are references in this essay to the duties we have to sustain and enrich our Country. A true Soldier of Christ recognizes and accepts responsibility for the parallel nature and extent of those duties and strives to meet or exceed those duties.

Commitment leads us to Courage ...

Courage

It takes courage to stand and be counted; to confront the serious problems facing our Holy Mother Church.

It takes courage to speak out to fellow Catholics; friends and family members; fellow parishioners, on the dangers facing the Church.

It takes courage to challenge the performance and the failures of the Bishops and Priests, Diocesan and Parish Administrators and Ministry Leaders who have strayed from the traditional teachings and principles of the Church and accepted, embraced and promoted so-called politically correct, touchy-feely theatrics and ceremonials to the extreme extent of supplanting revered, centuries old teachings, rituals and rites of the true Church with counterfeit forms of worship.

It takes courage to endure the ridicule that comes with the territory when you are engaged in the struggle to shine the light of truth and expose the many blatant and even heretical practices that are found in many Catholic Churches in the present day.

It takes courage to call to task the many Bishops, Clergy and Lay Persons who twist scripture to justify their complicity in criminal behavior by encouraging illegal immigration and harboring criminal trespassers in clear violation of the law of the land . . . all done under the masquerade of "helping the poor", when their activities are actually stealing the resources of communities and states that are paid for by hardworking Americans who themselves are made poorer as a result of such fraudulent and callous behavior in complete disregard of true Church teaching.

It takes courage to call attention to actions which indicate that the Church appears to ignore the fact that it exists in these countries from which the illegal invaders flow across our American borders, bringing crime and disease with them.

It takes courage to point out that the Catholic Church in those countries . . . the Same (One, Holy Catholic and Apostolic) Catholic Church as the American Catholic Church . . . with the exception that, at least in Mexico, there exists a high Church and a low Church, with the implications of that arrangement, *fails its people in those countries* and in utter disregard of the duty the Church has to protect and nourish them in the faith, *dumps* those unfortunate people onto the shoulders of Americans to deal with. The plight of the poor in Mexico and other areas of Central America is worthy of concern and consideration by American Catholics.

It takes courage to stand up and proclaim that the plight of those people, however, does not in any way, shape or form, justify either their abandonment by the Mexican and Central American Catholic Church or the American Church's promotion, support and participation of breaking the law of the land and bankrupting America's hard earned and generously shared resources in God's name. That is a shame and a disgrace. Worse than that, it is a gross insult to God!

The Church desperately needs Soldiers of Christ to rescue the Church from those who have been firmly engaged in its deconstruction and to rebuild it to its rightful glory and purity of purpose. The Catholic Church belongs to God.

Just as Jesus threw the money changers out of the Temple, we need to be Soldiers of Christ and throw the Imposters out of our Holy Mother Church

It takes Courage to stand up and be counted in the struggle to defend, restore and preserve our beloved Country. The same forces, organizations and movements that are at work on the deconstruction of our Church, are stealthily working to destroy America from within. These forces consist of a loosely formed and, in some cases, unconnected, array of enemies of the Church and America. Our enemies have repeatedly warned us of their plan to destroy us from within; loudly proclaimed that their efforts will not cease until their combined missions to destroy both the Church and the Nation are completed and America and the Church lie in ruins.

It takes courage to work every day to defeat our enemies; to establish and remain in continuous contact with your elected government representatives on all levels; to monitor the performance of School Boards and other higher learning institutions whose influence can and in many instances does constitute a threat to the development of our children. "Eternal vigilance" was long ago declared by Thomas Jefferson to be "the price of freedom". Never in our Nation's lifetime have those powerful words been truer than they are today.

It takes courage to rouse one's self to action; to get involved, join one of the Tea Party Patriot organizations or any one or more than one of the many other Patriotic grassroots organizations that are appearing in ever greater numbers all over the country, and to do all you can to make a difference in the work that lies before us in the desperate fight to save and Restore America.

It takes Courage.
Where do you stand? With Jefferson's words in mind and remembering that freedom is not free, and was purchased for all of us at enormous human cost, will you join today with all of the other patriotic Americans and devout Christians and do your part?

It takes courage.
Webster's American English Dictionary defines courage thus: **n: ability to conquer fear or despair.** That is concise and clearly to the point. I propose to you that one need not rise to the level of a hero to have courage. I believe, in fact, we are, each and every one of us, capable of being courageous.

Please look deeply into your mind, heart and spirit and ask yourself if you hear God's call to restore His Church and our Country.

You have the power given to you by the Holy Spirit, and you can do it.

A SPECIAL KIND OF DAY . . .
FEBRUARY 6, 2011

Donald J. Cole

Today, in America, we celebrate two distinctly American Phenomena. Today is Super Bowl Sunday. Over-arching that uniquely American Event is another Classic American Event: the 100th anniversary of the birth of Ronald Reagan, fortieth President of our United States of America.

For the football junkies, fanatics and authorities of all sorts, Super Bowl Sunday is what might be thought of as a "Football Holy Day Of Obligation". This is it! Today, it's the whole enchilada! For the 2010 Football season (and, yes, that's *FOOTBALL,* not *FUTBALL*) there is nothing else. Yes, I understand there is yet to be the Pro Bowl, but that doesn't stack up as the American Premiere Event the Super bowl is. Everything that is part of the Super Bowl extravaganza, from TV Ratings, to Beer Commercials, to Half-Time Show shenanigans, to Referees, to Color Commentators, to Play-by-Play Announcers; is elevated to the *Euphoric* heights of the whole Spectacle.

Prognosticators have been dueling for the past two weeks over who will win and by what score.

One predicts that Green Bay will win, 27 – 24 or maybe even 35 – 31. His Co-Prognosticator has Pittsburgh 27 – 24 or maybe even 35 – 31. *Excuse me?* For two weeks we have heard and read the opinions of the so-called expert analysts as they have dissected the talents, strengths, weaknesses, strategies, statistics and let's not forget the peeks into the behind-the-scenes intrigues that everyone *knows* will have an impact on the final outcome of the game on the field . . . Yeah, right.

Well, it is time to stop all of the foolishness. I am going to tell you how it ends, while you still have time to get online and bet the farm on it. This is serious business. Now, pay close attention. Pittsburgh has thirty-eight (38) players on their team who have played in a Super Bowl game. Green Bay has two(2) such players. Both teams are deserving of being in the Super Bowl. They are fairly evenly matched defensively. They are both capable of explosive (oops, is that a politically incorrect term ?) offensive play (You see, there's another of those bad words). But here, in fact, is how it ends: Are you ready? Wait for it . . . Pittsburgh - 31 . . .Green Bay – 14. (My fingers are crossed, just in case . . . well, you know.)

What elevates the whole experience of today's events ? There will be a pre-game tribute to Ronald Reagan that will give many Americans who never knew this great man an opportunity to learn about what made him what I personally consider to be the greatest President of the United States of America in the twentieth century. I am sure that on this day, President Reagan is enjoying his reward in Heaven on this 100th anniversary of his birth. I am a member of The Heritage Foundation, which was President Reagan's highest regarded think tank when he was President and is one of today's greatest repositories of Ronald Reagan's thoughts and writings in all of America. If you are not familiar with The Heritage Foundation I highly recommend you visit them at www.heritage.org. You may want to join us in the work ahead to restore the American virtues and values President Reagan so nobly reflected.

God Bless You, and God Bless America.

A Response to the SOTU Address of January 25, 2011

In one report I read, President Obama reportedly claimed in his State Of The Union address that he has "ordered a review of government regulations . . ." to reduce barriers to growth and investment . . .". "When we find rules that put an unnecessary burden on businesses, we will fix them.", he was quoted as saying. Oh, really, Mr. President?

I will state here, promptly and clearly, that I did not personally hear those words spoken in the televised coverage of the speech. I am long past the point of being capable of watching Mr. Obama's speeches without enduring a consequent powerful wave of nausea. There is no masochistic component in my DNA. Thus, I try not to subject myself to occasions or events that are likely to produce in me a gag reflex.

Forgive me if I sound particularly cynical but, you see, I'm approaching the 77th year of what I have planned to be a 100 year journey that I liken to a very long football game. So it is that I am now well into the fourth quarter and, having already faced the entire repertoire of the opposing team's playbook, I have developed instincts about what to expect to see for the remainder of the game.

Yes, that is just another way of saying I've been around the block a few times. But there are blocks and there are blocks. A few trips around the block in East or West Hampton, Long Island, New York, for example, would, in no way, resemble a few trips around the block in, say, Downtown Detroit, Michigan (if indeed, there is a Downtown Detroit anymore).

So what, then, should we take from Obama's pledge: "when we find rules that put an unnecessary burden on business, we will fix them". Does he want Americans to believe that, by ". . . we will fix them", he means "We will *remove* them"? Not likely, in my own humble opinion.

First and foremost, I do not believe Mr. Obama has, in fact, ordered the review of government regulations he claims to have ordered. Show me the Proof, Mr. President! I do not believe anything Mr. Obama says about anything. He has repeatedly shown himself to be a Liar . . . and at least one Congressman had the backbone to tell him that to his face (though he was ostracized for his courage to speak out against . . . a Liar, regardless of the Liar's name and position). Beyond not believing there was, in fact, any such order, I believe and submit to you, the translation of his "We will *fix* them" hinges on the operative word "unnecessary".

The "fix" I believe Obama and his cadre of czars and other such weirdo's will discover will be a concentrated effort that will transform those "unnecessary" burdens into "necessary" burdens.

I can visualize the report summary: "After an exhaustive review of government regulations, conducted at the request of President Obama, in his endless quest to foster growth and investment in American business, it has been determined that rules that had previously been believed to be unnecessary and burdensome on American business development have now been determined to be, not only *necessary*, but actually not as *stringent* as they need to be. Thus, the findings of the review ordered by His Excellency Barack Obama (Sorry, my bad) indicate that the rules are not burdensome or unnecessary, but must be made more stringent in order to "facilitate growth and investment in American business".

Though I elected to skip watching Obama's SOTU address, I have read and reflected on the full range of the content of his speech (written by I know not whom) and have found his message lacking any real connection with the needs and wishes of the majority of the American people. The man lives, I believe, in a separate universe, a dreamland, in which he is the glorious leader who is worshipped by his subjects.

You know, when you reflect on that, it sounds like a classic case of Mental Illness, doesn't it?

My personal strategy for the near term is to pray very hard for deliverance and for a surge in Patriotism and a substantial number of candidates for office who desire to work for the freedom, security and benefit of all Americans and to preserve the gifts of our Founders and all who came after them and did all they could, including sacrificing their lives to preserve our glorious Nation.

God bless and preserve America.

LEST WE FORGET

Donald J. Cole   December 7, 2010

On this December day two weeks before the first day of winter, America is at war, though it appears that, somehow, many in our beloved Nation do not seem to be aware of it. This war on radical Islamist terrorism will soon eclipse the Viet Nam war as America's longest war in our history.

As this war continues and ever growing numbers of our young warriors are killed and laid to rest, many so-called Americans are more concerned with trampling each other (to death in some cases) like savage animals at the local discount store or department store on "Black Friday", and otherwise conducting their lives like sub-human pigs.

Do a survey of the typical fare on television. Take a walk through your local Mall, and check out the parade of pierced, tattooed, slovenly freaks. My God, what has happened to us as a people? We are disintegrating as a Nation, destroying, or allowing to be destroyed, all that our Founders created and handed down to us . . . and which millions of our fellow Americans who came before us gave their full measure – their lives – defending this greatest, noblest and most generous nation that ever rose on this earth, to preserve it for us.

91

Can you see what is going on in America today and not question whether the enormous contributions and sacrifices of our forebears were worth the cost? Can you not question, in your heart, mind and soul, whether we, as a people, deserve all that we have? With all of the above said, it is not the primary reason why I write this short essay.

Sixty-nine years ago, on December 7, 1941 the Japanese conducted a sneak attack on the United States at our Naval base in Pearl Harbor, Hawaii in their insane quest to conquer and rule the world. That outrageous act, on a peaceful Sunday morning put the United States into World War II and set in motion the events of the following years that saw this great country save Europe and Asia. For the Japanese, their grandiose scheme brought them death and destruction of a never before seen magnitude and culminated in the spectacle of their humiliating , unconditional surrender to General Douglas MacArthur on the deck of the battleship USS Missouri in Tokyo Bay on September 2, 1945.

How many in America today, do you suppose, know much, if anything, about the significance of this day . . .December 7, and its importance on the stage of world history? How many in America today, do you suppose, would measure up to the contributions, suffering and sacrifices of those Americans who answered the call to duty on that long ago December day?

REMEMBER PEARL HARBOR . . .

Got A Split-Second To Spare?

Donald J. Cole , July 2009

The second half of the twentieth Century produced changes of astounding proportions in virtually every part of life on Earth.

The statement above is incontrovertible fact.

A high percentage of the changes; significant advances in science, technology, medicine, and more, grew out of research and development in the Soviets' and Americans' Space Programs. The extraordinary developments in the field of miniaturization illustrate the range and rate of changes wrought in the last fifty years of the twentieth millennium. Much of the change can be described, unequivocally, as beneficial to mankind.

But what of the changes that were not beneficial, but detrimental, to society? Cataloguing, evaluating and grading all of the changes of the past half century would be a monumental undertaking and is not the focus of this essay.

One major component was the ever increasing acceleration in the *rate of change* that continues, unabated, today. We are living in a time in which we are moving through life at warp speed.

There are two products of the changes of the past half-century that I want to address in this essay. Both are developments that greatly influence nearly all aspects of daily life, as I observe it. In order to address these *two products of change*, I will have to overcome the effects of the first to ensure that anyone will remain to read on for the discussion of the second.

The two products are these: First, *Attention Deficit*. Parallel to the rapid increases in the rate of change, we have seen, and continue to see, a corresponding, proportionate reduction in the attention span of vast numbers of people everywhere. The prevailing demand of what appears to be a majority of people today is for *instant everything*. No one wants to wait for anything. People today have no time to wait, no time even to speak. Everything is abbreviated and trivialized. Almost nothing seems to warrant an extended look; a review of the details; a thoughtful, reasoned, discussion of the merits.

The second product: An A*valanche of Greed*. Greed is pandemic and present in every strata of the general society, from the richest of the rich, to the poorest among us. Don't Think So? Stay with me, then, and I'll provide the details to prove the point.

These deleterious products of change feed each other and numb people to the details of the critical issues, threats, and dangers we face, as a consequence of them.

The old saying, "One thing leads to another", applies here. The rapidly increasing rate of change reaches across all facets of daily life.

Threats to Our Security and Freedom

Donald J. Cole, April 30, 2009
Cypress, TX

There is a ticking bomb sitting on your doorstep, right now, at this very moment. It is known as H.R. 45 and, if allowed to become law, would strip you and all of us of one of our most basic Constitutional rights.

Every Nation that ever fell to a Fascist Dictator, first saw its citizens stripped of their guns. When the secret Police come banging on – or breaking down – the door in the dead of night, it is hard to defend yourself if you do not have a weapon. We have a Constitutional right, under the Second Amendment of our Constition, to keep and bear arms. Our Founding Fathers understood the importance of that right.

PLEASE . . . Do not let a renegade government steal that right from you. Become an activist – Now - Today.

Support the organizations dedicated to protecting your Second Amendment rights. Communicate with your elected Congressmen and Congresswomen and your Senators, regularly – often if possible – by phone, mail and email. Demand that they work steadfastly to protect your Second Amendment rights and honor their sworn duty to preserve and protect the Constitution. Communicate, also, with lawmakers all over the country and warn them that you are watching how they vote and what they do. Make them aware that you will support any and all efforts to ensure the defeat of any Senator or Representative who fails to protect the Second Amendment. Keep informed, and do what you can to DEFEAT any and all such individuals.

Consider the fact that a million ten dollar contributions from all over the nation, to the campaign of the opponent of one of those elected individuals who fails or chooses not to protect the Second Amendment in any state, will get the job done. These elected officials, as a collective body on both sides of the aisle, have thumbed their noses at the people who elected them to bring the wishes of those same people to the House and the Senate and to do their jobs in a reflection of the wishes and interests of the districts and states they serve.

The cronyism and outright collusion of these political pretenders and absconders has gone on for far too long. It must be stopped. Politicians, Democrats and Republicans alike in large numbers, have cultivated their arrogance and elitist sense of superiority to a level that can no longer be tolerated. Many of them appear, by their words and actions (votes), to be saying, "To hell with the people, I'm here to look out for my own interest."

The Politicians must be shown, decisively and dramatically, that they will either do the will of the people they represent . . . or be dumped out of office – thrown out with the rest of the garbage.

A clear example of the problem is the insult to the American people and to the United States Constitution known as H.R. 45 introduced in recent days. That any U. S. Congressman has the unmitigated gall to even introduce such a Bill is, in itself, beyond redemption. This Bill would devastate your Second Amendment rights and, would likely make criminals of millions of law-abiding American citizens.

If that is what you are prepared to settle for, then do nothing. Others will shoulder your part of the burden. Yes, Burden. Every one of us has a responsibility to do our part to guard our freedoms. If we don't do that, eventually our freedom is lost. If we lose it, it will be lost forever. That is certainly not what I want for my grandchildren and their grandchildren. Please join your fellow Americans and let's get this country fixed.

GOD BLESS YOU AND YOUR FAMILY, AND GOD BLESS AMERICA.

The College Board's Masquerade

Donald J. Cole April 26, 2009
Cypress, TX

What first appeared to me to be, simply, a wrong-headed idea put forward by The College Board in choosing to lobby Congress to give tuition aid (. . .and a path to citizenship) to illegal aliens, upon further reflection, looks like a horse of a different color.[1]   No, I do not believe the move is what the Board would like us to believe it is. Rather, I believe the Board's attempt to get Congress to push through the ugly plan they propose is intended, not to educate the illegal invaders, but to swell the coffers of the 5,000 Member Institutions that comprise the Board, and the Board's lucrative SAT testing services with taxpayers' hard earned money.

This move is clearly just one of the latest illustrations of the rampant avarice and greed that now permeate every level of our society, and are destroying our country. The College Board now joins the ever-growing list of bottom feeders slithering up to the federal trough to suck up what they obviously believe to be their share of the life blood of our economy – Taxpayers' Dollars. Shame on these academic fakes!

"This is a new area for us, but it was an easy call," said a College Board Senior VP, Thomas W. Rudin. With classic Leftist Pin-headed logic, Rudin noted: the contradiction in which illegal immigrants who are legally entitled to a public education from kindergarten to high school [1] (*due to an egregious usurpation of legislative authority in a destructive 1982 Supreme Court decision - parenthetical comment mine*), suddenly hit barriers when applying to college, even when many are "honor roll students, athletes, class presidents and valedictorians."

Please, Mr. Rudin, you're getting me all choked up. Athletes? Class Presidents? Rudin ignores the real issue in question. These illegal invaders, despite a renegade Supreme Court decision, should not be entitled to *any* free public education paid for by the law-abiding citizens of this country, natural born and legally naturalized citizens alike. These illegal alien children, and the criminal parents who broke our laws and brought them here, should be deported back to their own countries and enrolled in their own country's schools.

Now, with college tuition rates rising to all-time highs, the College Board, in its transparent craving to grab a piece of the government money madness that is wrecking our economy, wants to elevate the criminal illegal's' status to that of preferential entitlement (there's that ugly word, again).

Who could possibly not believe that these illegal alien students are not more deserving than our own legal citizen students? *Well I, for one, Mr. Rudin.*

Quoting Bob Dane, a spokesman for American Immigration Reform, in his response to The College Board's announced plan, "The college Board is forgetting which side their bread is buttered: How can they purport to represent the interest of students while supporting legislation that promotes more competition from illegal aliens?"

"It's a massive amnesty effort being laid for this fall," Dane said. "Since many of these illegal aliens and their families are overwhelmingly on the lower end of the economic scale, they're going to take the lion's share of need-based financial aid."

Mr. Dane is correct in his assessment, as far as it goes. However, I submit that Mr. Dane and American Immigration Reform would better serve their cause, which I fully support, by shining the light on what I believe to be the true motivation of The College Board . . . not helping needy illegal alien students to obtain college financing . . . but employing that clever ruse to ultimately get Congress to provide The Board with enormous amounts of new dollars to Member Institutions and the ever expanding menu of College Board testing and preparation Products that bring lots of money into The College Board till.

This, as rightly proposed by Mr. Dane, would put the lion's share of need-based financial aid into the pockets of Illegal Aliens and punish deserving American citizens. But who is saying that The College Board cares anything about needy American students and their families? It's all about money - the money that will find its way to The College Board. Citizen or Illegal Alien, it doesn't matter to the College Board. It all spends the same.

Other of The College Board's findings included:

- About 360,000 illegal immigrants who have a high school degree[2] could qualify for the tuition aid.[3]
- Another 715,000 illegal immigrants between the ages of 5 and 17 would also benefit if they are motivated to finish high school and pursue a college degree. [3]
- who graduate from high school each year go to college.[3]

The College Board also claims: "roughly 10 states[1] which offer tuition aid to illegal immigrants generally saw increased college revenue by enrolling these

additional students, rather than financial burdens caused by an influx of immigrants (illegal) paying cheaper tuition.[4]

The Board also asserts: Their (illegal immigrants') ability to receive a higher education and move into better-paying jobs would help the U.S. economy in the form of increased tax revenue and consumer spending. [5]

[1] "College Board urges Congress to offer tuition aid, citizenship" by Hope Yen Associated Press, Chron.com, 4/21/09)

[2] High School "Degree"? We do not have High School "Degrees" in America. We have Diplomas. Or is the College Board thinking of Illegal invaders who get their High School "Degree" from their native country, then illegally sneak into America and, because there either are no colleges or only colleges for the wealthiest citizens in their native country, get in line for the Board proposed "tuition aid" . . . Oh, and let's not forget that bonus "path" to U.S. citizenship that is part of the sweetheart deal urged by the College Board.

[3] No attribution or authentication is given for these figures. There is no evidence of their validity.

[4] This dubious claim is made without any supporting data to authenticate it.

[5] A Utopian claim without merit. There is no evidence to support it. However, giving tuition aid to illegal trespassers would almost certainly mean denying it to legal American citizens.

A matter of Priorities

By Donald J. Cole,   April 2, 2009
Cypress, TX

Most Americans are aware of the enormous number of critical issues facing our nation today. I'm talking about matters of great importance covering virtually every vital area of concern, as they relate to what could come down to the very survival of our existence as a free nation and world leader.

We are at war on multiple fronts. Our banking and financial system are in shambles. The new administration of our federal government is driving us into socialism at warp speed, with barely a whimper from our elected Senators, Congressmen and Congresswomen.

The Federal government has turned GM (General Motors) into Government Motors. Congressman Barney Frank, one of the responsible parties for the mortgage industry collapse, and yet still holding a prominent chairmanship is trying to extend the reach of government   even deeper into the operations of private businesses. This is the same Barney Frank who was involved in the Congressional Page Male prostitution scandal.

Unemployment is rampant, running at all time highs, even as more and more jobs are shifted to offshore locations to feed the demand of the merchants of greed and avarice who run the companies that engage in the practice. Our enemies are attempting to destroy our currency and replace it with a so-called global currency.

The Socialist Obama regime intends to pass Cap & Trade legislation that, by Obama's own words, will cause energy prices to skyrocket.

The invasion of illegal aliens and illicit drugs are devouring huge amounts of states' money and infrastructure resources at the expense of hardworking American citizens.

The issues listed above are some, but by no means all, of the critical issues we are currently facing. Some of these ills have the very real potential to utterly destroy our beloved country and our freedom.

So what are the people we have sent to Washington to represent us and serve the interests of all Americans doing about all of the chaotic mess? Not much! The members of both houses appear more concerned with feathering their own nests and protecting their own selfish interests than repairing the damage that has been done to our country, largely as a result of the same two government bodies ' dismal failure to fulfill their duty to preserve and protect the interests of the

People. It is sickening to reflect on the miserable record our elected federal officials have amassed and the damage that has been inflicted on all Americans – and on generations of Americans to come.

As if my own level of disgust with these pathetic politicians was not high enough, this morning's newspaper provided me with information to raise my level of disgust for politicians even higher.

I read today the Senator John McCain, Republican from Arizona and Congressman Peter King, Republican from New York have found the time in their busy schedules, as they must surely be trying to deal with all of the serious issues listed above, to sponsor a resolution petitioning President Obama to posthumously pardon the Black former Heavyweight Boxer, Jack Johnson, who was convicted, in 1913, nearly one hundred years ago, of violating the Mann Act, for transporting an under age white woman across state lines for *consensual* sex. Johnson fled the country to France before he was sentenced. He was later defeated and lost the Heavyweight title, in 1915, to Jess Willard in Havana, Cuba. Johnson returned to the U.S. July 20, 1920 and surrendered to federal agents.

He was sent to the Federal Penitentiary at Leavenworth and served his one year sentence (rather a light sentence, I would submit, for a seven year fugitive from justice), and was released July 9, 1921.

On June 10, 1946, Johnson was reportedly refused service at a diner in Franklinton, NC, near Raleigh and was killed when he angrily sped off and crashed.

The race-baiters and dividers claim the pardon is appropriate; that Johnson was railroaded and he was only convicted because of his race. The facts, though, on which he was convicted, were that he broke the law and was found guilty for doing so. Johnson was, no doubt, hated by many white people of his time – and I believe by many good and decent black people as well – not for his color, but for the disrespectful, thuggish and decadent way he lived his life. There is nothing in the life of Jack Johnson to suggest he was a good and decent man; only a course and brutish fighter.

These two politicos, I can only consider to be either totally out of touch with what needs to be the business at hand, or simply stupid men. But, alas, sometimes seemingly stupid men may not be as stupid as they appear. Could it be that these two have some other agenda? Could there be some undisclosed motive for their action in requesting the blackish American President to pardon a thuggish black criminal for a sex crime he was convicted of nearly a hundred years ago?

I do not believe for one second that McCain and King are engaged in any noble cause to right a wrong. I believe these two politicians are pandering to the black racists in our society, who I believe constitute a larger percentage of black Americans than white racists are as a percentage of white Americans. It looks perfectly clear to me that McCain and King are addressing the demographics of where they can fortify their political ambitions. There is, indeed racism at large in America – as in every other part of the world. Too many of our politicians and so-called leaders are doing all they can to keep racism on both sides of the color line alive.

The article in this morning's paper reported that the reason why these two politicians who, instead of working full time on solving the real issues before them in these perilous times, could justify their efforts to make their petition is that we need to erase this act of racism. To that, I say hogwash!

If McCain and King can find no better way to occupy their time and use the resources of their office, all at the taxpayers' expense, they should pack up their stuff, get the hell out of the government and turn over their jobs to men who have America's interests as the basis of doing the job they are handsomely paid to do. Then, I would add: Good Riddance!

America At A Crossroads

Donald J. Cole 2008
Cypress, TX

Is there anyone in America who has not heard the phrase that is the title of this essay? Perhaps the phrase, so often pronounced at troubled times throughout our Nation's history, no longer resonates with most people. Let's do an analysis to see if we can find some new insight into what the phrase has meant in past times and what it means today.

Crossroads are intersections and there are numerous types of them. There is, of course, the basic type, that first comes to mind for most people, which is in the shape of a cross (+) or an (x). Another type of intersection takes the shape of the letter (Y), upright or inverted. There is an intersection shaped like the letter (T), also upright or inverted. Yet another type of intersection takes the shape of the letter (L), in its normal shape, or used backward, or inverted in either direction. There are also other varietal shapes of intersections or Crossroads. Whatever the type; the choice options are essentially the same.

In the early days of the American Colonies, before the Declaration of Independence, due to the abuses heaped upon the Colonists by the English Crown, the Colonists were faced with a crossroad, an intersection. That intersection required the Colonists to make a choice, as all intersections do in all cases. I would propose that the crossroad they faced is best represented by the cross shape. They had at least three clear options. They could simply continue on and endure the hardships the Crown imposed; they could simply refuse to obey the laws or pay the taxes and risk imprisonment and/or the loss of whatever they owned, or they could declare Independence and go to war . . . a simple array of options, with very complex possibilities for consequences. The Colonies were resolved to shed the oppression of the Crown and determined to be free. The Declaration was written and published. The Crown was put on notice that the Colonies would then move in a new direction of their own choosing.

Actions have consequences (another familiar old phrase). We know from history that the English Crown was as resolved to quash the upstart Colonists and punish them for their disobedience to the Crown. The Colonists were determined in their cause to obtain the freedom they believed they were entitled to. Thus, not just the Colonies, but both sides had to transit the Crossroad and the Revolutionary War ultimately resulted in America's Victory and Freedom.

Fast forward past several other, lesser, crossroads to that period in our Nation's life in the 1860's, when we faced yet another crossroad. This was more of an inverted Y type intersection, in that there were basically two sides, both part of this one Nation that wanted to move on different paths, but each side was resolved to fight to the death to determine which direction would

110

prevail. However, reality dictated that the Nation would move forward in only the direction chosen by the victorious side in the war. As we know from history, that crossroad led to the bloodiest war we have ever known, our War Between The States. The Nation survived that bloody nightmare and, at war's end, the two sides reunited and proceeded once again on the same path.

Two World Wars, WWI and WWII, the Korean War, the Vietnam War, and the First Gulf War brought America to numerous other crossroads, and today, in the midst of the deadly War On Terrorism, which can and should *more accurately* be called what it truly is: the *War Against Radical Islamic Terrorism* (a *World War* that, inexplicably, is not generally acknowledged to be a World War), we face in America yet another crossroads, one in which the course we take could result in the deadliest consequences America has ever faced – the ultimate destruction of our beloved country.

Most insidiously, the present crossroad is a double-edged sword. The threats from outside our borders are greatly amplified by the treasonous threats from within, which aid and comfort our external enemies. If we choose the wrong course at this crossroad, the America created by our Founders and preserved by the blood and sacrifice of our forebears may cease to exist, as have many other societies that came before us. This crossroad shows us the added dimension of a "Dead End" not far ahead if we continue beyond the crossroad before reaching the "Dead End" – our "Dead End".

One Party

ONE NATION, ONE PARTY . . .
INDIVISIBLE, UNDER GOD

Donald J. Cole, 2007
Cypress, TX

At the time of our Nation's birth, certain of the Founding Fathers, George Washington and John Adams among their number, did not favor a Party system for our political process. They saw the potential for a Party system to have a divisive effect on the new government of the Country.

The wisdom of those of the Founders who did not favor the Party system is clearly confirmed in the light of our present political condition. We are a nation polarized by the entrenched divisions of the Democrat and Republican Parties.

It is time for America and Americans to wake up and heed the lessons of history. Time and again, as Societies, Empires, Kingdoms, and Nations have crumbled into the debris of earth's human history, the truth of the lesson that "A house divided against itself cannot long stand" has been ignored with catastrophic consequences.

We are at a crossroads. The future is always uncertain. The continued survival, prosperity, and development of our great country depend upon our ability to see, and our willingness to address and solve, threats to our existence.

To that end, we must eliminate the cancer of division that has seized our national political process. The divided ideologies between the Parties have exploded over many decades, changing what once was heated debate . . . to acrimony . . .and now to unadulterated hatred.

With the passage of each of the last four decades in particular, the division within our country – our house – has grown exponentially. Our very system of government is threatened.

Our judicial system is in serious disarray, with activist renegade judges making, rather than interpreting the laws of the land.

It is time for America to dispose of the Party system, and replace it with a No Party system.

Oh, I can hear the outcry from Party loyalists on both sides. But I propose that an honest, unbiased analysis supports the abolition of Political Parties. Taking such action will enable the nation to restore the greatness to our political system that has been lost; subordinated to the sacrificial altar of Party priorities over National interest.

Certainly, one of the biggest obstacles to disposing of the Party system, in favor of a No Party election process, is money. The other major obstacle is Power. The institutional structures of both Parties control enormous amounts of money, and wield great power. Many people would say it is impossible now to dislodge and dismantle these powerful institutions.

There were many who said, during the birth of our Nation, that such an unprecedented form of government could not, and would not, be created. But this Nation and the incomparable freedoms of its government was indeed created, and for more than two hundred years flourished. However, any serious student of history cannot fail to see that the last forty-plus years have brought serious erosion. There are cracks in the institutional foundation of our noble form of government. To ignore these facts is dangerous and foolhardy.

Our forebears secured for us and for posterity, the greatest creation of government ever devised in the in the entire history of the world. We are, each and every one of us Americans, obliged to protect and preserve their great gift to us, purchased at a very high cost.

I accept my personal responsibility to meet my obligation, (and borrowing the words of a former U.S.

President I did not vote for) spare no effort, bear any burden, do everything I can do, to preserve the great gift of our Founding Fathers. I owe, we all owe, no less to the Founders and all who came after them and before us and made every manner of sacrifice and contribution to make this Nation endure.

To those who say it would be impossible to dismantle the entrenched Party system, I say it is not. Nothing is impossible.

I call upon the grace of our Almighty God and Creator, under Whose divine guidance and providence, the Founding Fathers so eloquently professed their profound faith and their eternal trust.

I'm Giving Up Watermelon For Lent

Donald J. Cole, 2008
Cypress, TX

I'm giving up Watermelon for Lent – again. That's what I have done (successfully, I might add) for the past few years. Saying you were giving up watermelon for Lent used to bring a more incredulous reaction when you said it, because watermelon was never in season during Lent. Now, it's a different story. These days, you can find watermelon in the markets year-round. So, today, watermelon is something that one *actually could* give up for Lent, though there would still be the perception by most that it was not much to give up. For me, it is a symbolic component of my Lenten observance.

But, before you write me off as some sort of Kook, focus on the operative word here: "component", and grant me a few more minutes of your attention to describe the totality of my Lenten observance. Allow me to explain the rationale for and relevance of the "watermelon component'.

You see, it struck me one Lenten day that all of this "what are you giving up for Lent?" business missed the real point of the Lenten season. In a heartbeat, I was

116

confronted by the realization that the Lenten habits I had cultivated since early childhood were more for and about me than my Savior.

As a young child, I learned that the Lenten season was a time for repenting and sacrifice. In those days of long ago, the sacrifice part was made simple for us kids. We were given little cardboard "mite boxes" to fold into shape and glue together. The little box, when completed, was about 1.5" thick, 3" high, and 4" long, and featured a coin slot on the top. We were encouraged to put coins into the box (mostly spare pennies in those days when we received a weekly allowance of ten cents) throughout the Lenten season. The Mite Boxes were then turned in to Church on Good Friday and the money was given to the foreign missions for the poor. It was a nice way to help a child learn the lessons of sacrifice and charity. And the practice produced, in addition to those lessons for the children, tangible financial aid to the poor in remote parts of the world.

The Repentance part was a more abstract concept to understand for a young child who didn't have much of a list of transgressions for which to repent. Thus, at some point, someone, somewhere developed the idea of giving up something that gave one pleasure or satisfaction , for the period of Lent, and "offering it up" as a way to repent for our sins. Once it was established, the practice quickly became a tradition.

And then the competition commenced.

Children and adults, alike, seemed to be bent on outdoing each other's Lenten sacrifices. "I'm giving up candy", one kid would say. "Well, I'm giving up candy and ice cream", the friend would counter. One adult male would tell his pals, "I'm giving up my usual glass of wine with dinner", only to hear one of his buddies say, "yeah, that's nice, but I'm giving up all drinking (alcohol) for Lent".

Okay, then, we can see the competition here. Is it good; bad? In general it is probably not bad for these kids and adults to want to do more to sacrifice, and in doing so, there is certainly something to be gained. Sacrifice, after all, is sacrifice. But what is the motivation for the competition? Is it to outdo your friends and, thus, be somehow a little better than them? Or is the motive to do more to make up for your own failures and shortcomings and truly offer a greater sacrifice to God for repentance of your sins and a sincere desire to better serve Him? Only the individual and God know the answer to these questions. It is easy, though, to find yourself doing good things for the wrongs reasons. That does not negate the good. But, neither does it elevate the good to its highest level.

With all of these thoughts in mind, I came to the conclusion that I didn't think God was completely satisfied with the way I had been observing Lent. I had a small epiphany. I decided that my focus was in the wrong place; that, instead of trying to "give up" something for Lent, I should focus, instead on "Doing", instead of "Not Doing".

I began telling people I was giving up watermelon for Lent, more as a joke, than anything else. It always got a reaction. The typical reaction, usually eye popping disbelief, gave me an opportunity to expand a bit and explain that I have refocused my Lenten observance. Instead of "giving up" this or that, I have chosen instead, to perform random acts of kindness, as many times a day to as many people I can throughout the Lenten season. The possibilities are almost limitless. It doesn't matter how rich or poor you are, or any of those extraneous factors. It can be as simple as smiling and saying, "hello", or "God bless you" to a stranger you may never see again.

On one occasion, I observed a young lady at a restaurant reading her Bible as she ate her lunch. She was black, I am white. With all the racial tension in the world, I wanted to reach out, do a small thing to neutralize one tiny bit of that tension and, at the same time, lift another person's spirits. I leaned over toward her and said, "Excuse me Miss". She looked up at me and before she could say anything, I continued, "I see you are reading your Bible. Do you know what will happen to you if you keep doing that?" She thought for a moment, then with a noticeable sparkle in her eyes, she replied, "I'll go to Heaven". I was speechless for a moment (something very uncommon for me), then I said, "Yes, indeed you will, and you'll probably take many others with you."

She said, very quietly, "Thank you." I replied, "And thank you", and left to go on with the rest of my day. It was an awesome experience, I think, for both of us.

So, I give up watermelon every year for Lent (I try to deny myself other special things from time to time, as well), but my real focus now, for Lent, is "Doing".

Should you decide to try "Doing" things for Lent, as I do, I think you will feel as good about it as I do. And you will discover, as I did, that the practice will carry over into the rest of the year.

Jesus ... The Reason For The Season

Donald J. Cole,   December, 2007
Cypress, TX

We are, tonight, about halfway through the Season of Advent. I'm sure most of us here have been busy these past days and weeks of Advent preparing to celebrate the anniversary of the birth of our Lord, Jesus Christ. And there are many ways in which we make our preparations for this Joyous Holy Day.

In our jobs, we try to get loose ends tied off, clear the decks of all of those complicating issues that might crop up to infringe upon the time we plan to spend with family and friends throughout the so-called Holiday Season.

At home there are many things to take care of. The house gets spruced up for anticipated visits by friends and family. There are decorations to be put up inside the house and outside – Christmas Trees festooned with beautiful ornaments and glowing with an array of lights; Wreaths and garlands of evergreens (real or imitation) for doors and walls and banisters and balconies and mantels; lighting to adorn the eaves of the house and lighted displays of all sorts of descriptions to ring the whole house in the "Spirit" of the season.

There would appear to be no end to the variety of lawn displays. You can see herds of Reindeer, hoards of Santas and Snowmen and Angels, blowing long Trumpets . . . and if you look hard enough you will occasionally even see a lighted Nativity Scene in a front yard here or there.

We put up a lighted Nativity scene display in our front yard every year. It consists of just five components, Mary, Joseph, a crib, the infant Jesus, and a lighted star that we place above our little scene on the trunk of one of our big pine trees. The little set is old. It's made of molded and painted plastic, that forms the figures. There is a light inside each figure to illuminate it. Some people think the kind of little display we have looks cheap. Well, the truth is that the little set was purchased years ago for a cheap price. But, at the time, we wanted to put out a Nativity scene display to call the attention of all who saw it that this was, after all, what Christmas was really about, and it was all we could afford to buy at the time.

Over the years Patsy and I have said many times to each other that we should try to find a nicer set. Then after Christmas is over and the decorations are taken down and stored away we forget until the following year when we always seem to be trying to catch up to our neighbors who somehow manage to find the time to get their decorations up weeks before us. This year was to be different. I was determined to get ahead of the decorating curve and upgrade our Nativity set, too. But that was before the furnace went out and before the water pump, thermostat and harmonic balancer went out on my Jeep and, you guessed it, the schedule went out the window.

For the past several days, I have searched for a new Nativity set. There were some beautiful ones at Sam's or Costco back just before Halloween – *or it might have been July or August*, I really can't recall. All I remember is that they were there. They are no longer there – or anywhere else either. I tried six stores: Sam's, Costco, Home Depot, Lowe's, Wal Mart, and Target. Target was the last store I tried, yesterday, Sunday, the twelfth of December.

The Target experience was a depressing revelation for me. After searching all over the department and finding nothing I asked a clerk, or whatever name they give these days to the people who walk around in those stores. I said, "Do y'all not have any outdoor Nativity sets for sale?" The kid looked to be around eighteen years old. He said, "A what?".   "A Nativity set", I replied. When he asked, "What's that? ", I knew we had nothing else to talk about.

I left the store feeling pretty depressed, partly because I couldn't find a new Nativity Set, of course. But hearing that kid who appeared to be old enough to vote tell me he didn't know what a Nativity Set was, really was a low point. And I spent some time reflecting on that and on the fact that the stores are loaded down with every kind of secular display one can imagine – and some you can't imagine (there is a guy down the street from me who has, as a prominent part of his yard display, an orange and white lighted longhorn steer).

We Catholics and Christians of all denominations have a serious problem on our hands. The avalanche of secularism is growing. How far will it go before we draw the line in the sand?

My day was rescued though, and my spirits renewed, when Patsy and I went to Jones Hall last night to see the Houston Symphony's "A Very Merry Pops". The show had some of the usual commercial Christmas songs, Rudolph, etc. But the Highlight of the show was its focus on the real reason for the season. There was a narration interwoven with the music and ending with the story, "One Solitary Life" - An essay on the life of Jesus Christ

I will close this program tonight with a humorous story the Maestro told about a man who was interviewing for a job as a Department Store Santa. The Manager said he wanted to be sure he hired the right person for the job. He told the applicant that since he'd be representing the store to all of the children and their parents, it was important that the person to be hired for the job be intelligent and able to think quickly.

"I have a short test and would like you to answer a few questions, if you don't mind" he asked the candidate. The man agreed. "How many days of the week begin with the letter T?", asked the manager. The candidate thought it over for a brief moment and said "Four". "How'd you get that" asked the manager. "Well, there's Tuesday, Thursday, Today, and Tomorrow", came the reply. "Okay, then, I'll give you that one" the manager said.

"Now, How many seconds are there in a year?" "Twelve", came the Candidate's quick reply. "Well, how in the world did you come up with that", asked the manager. "Simple", said the man, "There's January second, February second and so on all the way through December, twelve in all". "Alright, I suppose I can accept that.

Now please tell me how many D's are in the Christmas Carol The Little Drummer Boy? The man closed his eyes and began to think about the question. It was obvious that he was really working on it. His lips were moving, finger bouncing around as if counting . . . then finally the man gave his answer, "Four hundred and Seventy-two", he said.

"What ? How in Heaven's name did you ever come up with such an answer? ", the manager asked. "Well", said the man, "it goes – Dee Dee Dee Dee, Dee, Dee Dee   Dee   .   .   .   .   .   .   "

Please have a Merry Christmas. And spread the word, as far and wide as you can . . .

Jesus is the Reason for the Season.

In Observance of Memorial Day

Donald J. Cole , May 24, 2007
Cypress, TX

From the first days of the stirrings of liberty and justice for all that led to the founding of our much blessed nation, through the decades and centuries up to this day, more than a million devoted, patriotic American men and women, paid the ultimate price; sacrificed their very lives in the cause of creating and preserving our great nation and the principles for which it stands. More than one million lives given to purchase the freedom and opportunity that each one of us enjoys, here, tonight.

What an enormous debt we owe to all of those good people.

Next Monday, May 28, 2007, is designated as the day on which we conduct our Memorial Day observance. I have seen the characteristics of this national day of observance change radically over the span of my own lifetime. I recall it to have always been a day of celebration, with parades and speeches and food and yes, games too. But central to the activities of the day was always the core of solemn reflection and gratitude for the great sacrifices of those who made possible our own lives of freedom. Indeed, what we celebrated was the pure gift from those we honored and our own pure gratitude for their gift to us.

The tone and tenor of the day have changed. The solemnity of the occasion seems almost no longer to exist for many people, the celebration, in these times, seems more to be for the extra profits the merchants anticipate and the bargains to be grabbed by the general public at the mall.

In the midst of all the fun and activities of the day, all that seems to be available for the true reason for the occasion is a three or four minute sound bite on the evening's TV newscasts that show small groups of people (probably fewer than one half of one percent of the total local population) conducting a handful of memorial services at area churches and cemeteries.

I respectfully suggest and invite each of you to dedicate your celebration on Monday to the real reason for the day and to make participation in a memorial service a vital part of your overall observance and your family's celebration. And may god continue to shower his blessings on our country and our families.

Save Our Nation . . . Save Our Church

Donald J. Cole, 2006
Cypress, TX

Prior to Vatican II, one could attend Mass anywhere in the world and experience the same rites, rituals, and prayers in every Roman Catholic Church with few, if any, minor differences. The Latin of the Mass provided a constancy that is not present from one parish to another today. The Mass in those days inspired reverence and gave one the comforting sense, the tangible familiarity and awareness of the timelessness of our Catholic Faith and tradition.

Then came the disaster known as the Second Vatican Council, commonly known today as "Vatican II".

Vatican II coincided with the emergence of the so-called "Sexual Revolution" and the "Drug Culture" of the 60's and 70's and the venom of the so-called "Feminist Movement" which has done more than anything in human history to de-feminize women and girls, and has gravely injured the Church.

Can any honest Catholic look at the Church today and truthfully say he or she believes the Church is better and healthier now than in pre-Vatican II times? The Church has been devastated by the monumental loss of Vocations. We have severe shortages of Priests. Religious Brothers and Nuns, who staffed schools and hospitals, taught our children in the Catholic Schools that were a part of nearly all parishes, are almost non-existent in the Church today. How? Why? I will tell you how and why. But I believe that, in your heart, you already know how and why.

The bungling, utopian architects and engineers of Vatican II, who proclaimed a desire to throw open the windows and doors of our Church to let in fresh air and open us up to the world, sorely lacked the vision and wisdom to see what their glorious delusion would actually accomplish. The ineptness of the well-intentioned individuals among their numbers exposed them to the wicked wiles and deceits of the ones among them who were, indeed, NOT well intentioned. Those who had long harbored the desire for personal power lost no time setting about the business of undermining the most revered traditions and rites of the beautiful Church that Jesus established on this earth more than two thousand years ago.

No, my dear friends, Vatican II did not let in any fresh air. Rather, Vatican II allowed all manner of pollution and poison into our Church, and caused astonishing injury over the last four decades that will take many decades to repair. Our Church infrastructure is riddled with infiltrators who reject true Catholic teaching and values. These people – Clergy and Lay Persons – are fervently working every day to dismantle the Church and create, in its place, something that is anything but orthodox Roman Catholic. And they are good at what they are doing. They conceal and camouflage their anti-Catholic activities under the guise of "Social Justice" and "Service to the Poor" among other facades.

Look around you. Can you not see the parallels between what is going on in both our Church and our Country? Do you believe it is just coincidence that the demise of our National morality commenced at the same time as the demise of the sacred traditions and values . . . yes, values . . . in our Church? It is not an accident. The people in our government who present themselves as "Catholics" and not only support such practices as "partial birth abortion" (which is really nothing more than the cold blooded murder of a living, partially born CHILD) but they vigorously PROMOTE such evils. *Catholics?* **Catholics?** They say so.

Their counterparts within the infrastructure of our Church are there in great numbers doing their works of sabotage in usually more subtle ways. The New Mass in the 60's brought with it all sorts of changes, not just changing the language to the vernacular. Almost overnight, when viewed in the context of the entire history of the Church, we were instructed that the "sacrificial" tone of the "Old" Mass made people feel uncomfortable which, we were informed, was a "downer".

So, in order to open the windows and doors to let in fresh air, the Mass – the Holy Sacrifice of the Mass – was transformed into the "Celebration of the Eucharist".

Suddenly we were free of the "dreariness" of our beautiful Mass, and released from mournful burdens of guilt we had previously been required to bear. All sorts of utopian groups and movements appeared, to shepherd us into the new light.

One of the major "discoveries" of the new era was that we had to incorporate innovative changes, not just to the "language" of the Mass but also to the sound and sight aspects. A "Lector" in the 60's served as both "reader" and "cantor". Having served for these forty odd years as a Lector I have many recollections of changes. Soon after the New Mass was installed, it became important to many of the Clergy, and their new cadres of lay-persons who would help bring the Church into the new era, to add new wrinkles to the Mass that would make it "appeal to more people".

Thus, we saw the emergence of the "Folk Mass" among other things. Guitars sprang up in Parishes, like weeds in a garden, and the "Flower Children" of the times were supposed to be drawn into the Church by this wonderful new version of what had once been embraced as the Holy Sacrifice of the Mass. The guitars are still around in many parishes along with drums, tambourines and the like, to add entertainment value to the present day "Eucharistic Celebration".

The newly formed "Parish Councils" that would "assist" Father with the running of the Parish filled up with members eager to "help" Father and bring fresh ideas into the everyday life of the Church. The Parish Councils created other organizations to "help". Liturgy Committees became essential to the life of a Parish, though I have never been able to come up with a good reason why.

In my own experience as a Lector, the Liturgy Committee in my parish of the time in the late 60's and early 70's established a new format in which the Lector, immediately before the start of Mass, would read to the congregation the "Theme" for the day's Celebration. Then, immediately preceding each of the readings, the Lector was required to read to the congregation a brief explanation of what the Reading from Holy Scripture meant. So it was, that the Liturgy Committee, a small group of parishioners, wrote these introductory commentaries which the Lector was required to read, and presumed to be capable and have the authority to tell the congregation "what the Scriptural Passages meant".

To add further insult, the Pastor, at one point purchased a weekly cassette tape program that had the readings for each particular Sunday recorded on it. The speaker on the tapes had a very dynamic, theatrically trained voice and perfect diction. He was probably a professional actor or media commentator who stumbled onto a new source for a cash stream. He might even have been Christian, possibly even Catholic. The routine was that the Lectors were to play the tape several times and "rehearse" along with it making a best effort to mimic the speaker on the tape.

I had been a Lector for eleven years when the Pastor, with the "help" of the Liturgy Committee installed this program and I simply balked and refused to use the tapes. To the present day, I study the reading(s) on the evening before I am to read. I read through them a few times silently and a few times aloud to both familiarize myself with the reading(s) and to determine what God is saying to me through the words of scripture. Then, at Mass, I give my best effort to proclaim the words of Scripture as sincerely and clearly as I am able.

I do not believe any Lay Person should presume to be capable of instructing another as to what a particular passage of scripture means. I believe the message and meaning one receives from a scriptural passage – words written under Divine inspiration – are personal to each individual. I may hear or read a particular passage today and derive a specific message and meaning from it that applies to me and my life and my relationship with my Savior. On a future day and time, I may read or hear that same passage and receive from it a very different message and meaning. On both of those occasions, if you hear or read the identical passage, the message and meaning you receive may be very different from mine. Dare I presume to tell you what God wants you to hear and learn from any sacred writing? I dare not.

A brief aside here:

Not long after installation of the tape program, I determined it was time for me to step aside. The things I was seeing and hearing in the Church were very disturbing for me and I could not bring myself to accept these activities and declarations of Lay People whom I believed did not have true Catholic teaching and values as their motives.

On the day when I last read in that Parish, I took a few moments to speak to the congregation prior to the beginning of Mass about my decision to step aside as a Lector. I expressed my sincere gratitude for having had the privilege and the blessings of proclaiming God's word for eleven years. I did not want to create any problems for anyone or express any bad feelings.

What I said, as closely as I can recall my words, was: "For eleven years I have had the enormous privilege and blessing of standing at this Lectern and proclaiming Holy Scripture to you, my fellow parishioners. I truly hope that my reading of the Word was a positive part of your experience of the Mass. We have seen many changes in our Church since that change that created the position of Lector that has been a precious gift for me. Some of the subsequent changes, I believe, have been good for our Church. Some, I believe in my own perception of right and wrong, have not. What is important now is that the relentless pace of change in our Church is more than I am able to manage without being distracted from my duty and responsibility as a proclaimer of the Holy Scriptures. I find myself now in a position like the old dog in the well-known proverb. It's time for me to move along. Thank you all for the many kindnesses you have extended to me. God bless you."

What happened next stunned and embarrassed me. The entire congregation broke into applause for what was, to me, a painfully long time. I had not anticipated such a reaction to my words. One would rarely, if ever, hear clapping in a Catholic Church at the start of Mass. In retrospect I believe the spontaneous response happened because my words touched feelings of their own that matched the feelings of frustration and disappointment that I had so awkwardly addressed in my words. Whatever the dynamic of the moment, it was very uncomfortable for me. I had consciously wanted only to express my sincere thanks for having had the honor and the blessing of being a Lector and for the many kindnesses my fellow parishioners had shown me over the years.

Looking back, I realize that the alienation and frustration; the deep disappointment I felt from the radical changes in our Liturgy and traditions clearly showed through in the words I spoke that morning. At the time, my own assessment of the effects of the radical changes we were seeing in the Church, was that those who had swept into Church Hierarchy power in the wake of Vatican II were doing everything they could to trivialize the Church, its teachings and traditions. I hold to that assessment to this day. But today I believe the trivialization is far worse than it was then.

I cannot look at the problems facing our Church today without clearly seeing the parallels between or Church and our Country. In my view, the cancer that is eating away the vitals of our Church is directly linked with the cancer that is destroying our Nation.

Here are a few comparisons. Read them and reflect on them. Then judge for yourself if these conditions and issues represent a threat or a danger to Holy Mother Church.

- Several States have passed laws allowing same sex marriage. Other States and local governmental jurisdictions have enacted laws granting spousal rights and benefits to cohabitating homosexuals and lesbians.

- Adoption laws, rules and procedures have, in numerous places, been altered to allow homosexual or lesbian individuals or couples to adopt children – children who are neither old enough to even begin to know or understand the implications of such arrangements, nor able to reject for themselves, any such living conditions inflicted upon them by a system that has power over their young lives.

- Recent news reports tell, in glowing terms, that "advances" in science indicate that new processes may soon make it possible for a woman to have a child totally without the participation of a man – not even requiring some form of artificial insemination.

- This embryonic stem cell research (itself an affront to God).

OUR CHRUCH –
- Consider the fact that a Catholic Church affiliated organization – Catholic Charities of Boston – blatantly arranged numerous adoptions of children by openly homosexual same sex couples, and brazenly claimed to justify those adoptions and the practice, claiming that they (Catholic Charities of Boston) found those homosexual couples offered a more loving environment to the children.

- Consider the fact that an organization calling itself "Couples For Christ", claiming in parish bulletins and other Church publications, to be "Recognized" by the Vatican invites, among others, married couples, singles and even people who are living together and not married, to join their organization and attend meetings held in Catholic Church parish facilities.

Do you see any parallel? Do you believe there is nothing of concern . . .to our Country . . .to our Church? Is this all simply benign coincidence? Please read on . . .

OUR NATION –

- Since 1973, an American Holocaust has relentlessly slaughtered innocent unborn children, more than forty million of these victims of the Godless pursuit of the so-called "Women's Right To Choose". Fortunately, the absolute horror of "Partial Birth Abortion" has now been stopped and the ban was upheld by a recent Supreme Court Decision. But Abortion as a means of contraception, genetic selection, and mindless base selfishness rages on, as politicians – including many despicable, self-proclaimed Catholic politicians, not only support – but aggressively promote – the evil culture of death.

OUR CHURCH –

- Too many of our Church Leaders, who should be waging a non-stop war against the brutal culture of death, manage little more than a mild mannered whimper – a "Now you mustn't do that" kind of response to the slaughter. The American Conference of Catholic Bishops, the Princes of the American Catholic Church who, by now should have publicly and prominently declared the excommunication from the Catholic Church of every one of the Counterfeit Catholic Politicians who so openly and brazenly – even to the point of issuing a public statement last year, warning the Church to butt-out – mock the Church and it's teachings.

Is there any parallel here? Is there even a shred of evidence that both our Nation and our Church are in Dire Straits?" Search your Soul and find the answer for yourself . . . and for the Church.

Killing The American Dream

Donald J. Cole, June 30, 2006
Cypress, TX

RECOGNIZING THE THREAT OF OUT OF CONTROL CORPORATE EXECUTIVE COMPENSATION

In the year 2005, the average annual salary for Corporate CEO's (defined as: the sum of salary, bonus, value of restricted stock at grant, and other long-term incentive award payments.[1]) was $10,982,000.00. That salary was 262 times the average worker's salary (defined as: the hourly wage of production and nonsupervisory workers, assuming the economy-wide ratio of compensation to wages and a full-time, year-round job[1]). Thus, the average worker's salary in 2005 was $41,916.00. Thus, with 260 work days per year, an average worker's annual salary was equal to ONE DAY of the CEO's pay.

In the year 1965, the average annual salary for Corporate CEO's was 24 times the average worker's salary. The disparity between average CEO salaries and average worker's salaries continued to grow until the difference was an astonishing 300 times, in the year

140

2000. The difference dropped from 2000 to 2002 to 143 times difference, rising again from 2002 to 2005 to the 262 times spread between the two average levels shown above.

Consider this fact: from 1965 to 2005, the CEO salaries grew from 24 times that of the average worker to 262 times difference. In other words, in 2005, average CEO's were enjoying a salary advantage over average workers 238 times greater than in 1965. That is a stunning amount of growth. What is the justification for such disparity? Can anyone believe average worker's had anything to do with the CEO's salaries?

Since CEO's salaries are reputed to be (though often are not) the product of how well the CEO runs the company, and the earnings his leadership generates; and since those earnings are mostly the result of the ideas, innovations and generally the work output of the workers in the company, why then, did not the workers' salaries grow on a scale even remotely similar to that of the CEO? Is this enormous disparity in compensation between CEOs and average company workers a function of basic Capitalism? Not in my view, it isn't. Is it reasonable or prudent to assume that paying a CEO (who is, after all, an employee of the company) a compensation package 262 times that of the average employee of the company is somehow conducive to increasing performance by all of the average employees?

Is it reasonable or prudent to assume that paying the CEO 262 times more than the company's average worker's earnings is somehow a good deal for the company's **stockholders**?

The American Dream, as I learned it, could roughly be defined as the opportunity to apply one's self to a life of work in whatever field of endeavor that would lead to achieving goals and rewards in proportion to the effort of the individual (with some allowances for occasional extra rewards as a result of what might be called lucky breaks).

As I view the American Dream, in the context of today's society, I see the practice of paying CEOs 262 times as much as a company's average worker as a killer of the American Dream.

It is not Capitalism!

It is the deconstruction of Capitalism. The practitioners of avarice and greed, despite what some say to the contrary, are the enemies of Capitalism, as well as agents of the destruction of the true American Way.

The words of Stanley Marcus, one of the founders of Nieman-Marcus Stores, a premiere Capitalist if ever there was one, have stayed in my mind since the day I read them many years ago in an interview Mr. Marcus gave to Inc. Magazine: . . ."*When a company goes public, it loses its Corporate Soul.*"   Indeed, Mr.

Marcus, and the number of lost corporate souls continues growing.

[1] Source; MSN Money, EPI citation, June 27, 2006

The American Media
... Then and Now

Donald J. Cole, March, 2006
Cypress, TX

Back in the old days, when I was growing up in Brooklyn, during the war years of the 1940's the Media in America were very different from what we have today. There were numerous news commentators on radio - we didn't have television , at least not in my home, until late 1949. But the radio news commentators like Walter Winchell, with his customary greeting of, **"Good evening Mr. And Mrs. America, and all the ships at sea"**, and either Gabriel Heater or H. V. Kaltenborn— not sure which—who always opened his broadcast with the words, **"There's good news tonight"**

They were very different times, back then . . . and not easy times. The world was at war. There was much danger, hardship, suffering and sacrifice for all Americans, rich and poor alike. Sons, brothers, husbands, fathers, uncles went away to war, leaving friends and loved ones behind to worry and hope and, of course, to pray. Many of those Americans did not come home.

One of the notable things about the media people of that era was that they were *patriotic* Americans; proud of our country, and of the people who lived, without

144

whining, with the hardships of the times.

Today the world is also at war. But it is a different kind of war, and we seem to have as many enemies within as we do beyond our borders. The battle that rages on reaches into every corner of our lives. Yet we average Americans are not forced to sacrifice and endure hardships like the old days.

The media people seem determined to do anything but support our country. Unlike those old WWII days when a commentator could always find and proclaim that there was **"good news tonight"**

Today's media choose not to find and report good news about America. But there is, indeed, good news tonight **and I will tell you what it is:** It is an awakening of the Real American Spirit among a growing number of our people. That awakening is what will get us through these terrible times that threaten to destroy America.

Make no mistake about the very real threats to our continued existence as the Greatest Nation on Earth . . . they are not idle threats to be taken lightly. But the good news is that there are enough numbers of us who will do what must be done to overcome the threats to us and America Will Prevail. If America failed and crumbled . . . the rest of the world would crumble in our wake.

THAT WILL NEVER HAPPEN!

Parallels

Donald J. Cole, 2005
Cypress, TX

In a recent conversation with a friend about some of the vexing problems of our times, I recalled for my friend the words spoken by Stanley Marcus, one of the Neiman Marcus Department Stores' founders, in an interview for INC. Magazine. The interviewer wanted Mr. Marcus' thoughts and observations on the state of the department store industry, at the time of the interview, which occurred about twenty years ago.

Mr. Marcus lamented the fact that department stores had all become too much alike. One could no longer walk into a store and know, by its appearance and presentation, which store it was. The stores, he told the interviewer, had become mirror images of each other – and carried the same merchandise, all of which was of lower quality. The marketing, sales, and merchandising were all the same. Buyers no longer set foot on the sales floor, and wouldn't dream of asking the sales clerks what kind of merchandise their customers were asking for. When asked to explain the phenomenon, Mr. Marcus gave an astounding reply, telling the interviewer that all of these department stores going public was at the core of the problem.

"When a company goes public", Mr. Marcus said, "It loses its Corporate Soul". What a remarkable observation from a man in the all time upper echelon of the world of commerce; a consummate capitalist, who knew more than most what capitalism really is – or should be. Instead of conducting business to provide the finest possible products at fair prices, that would please the customers and give the business a fair – even handsome return, the giant , modern day, publicly traded department store holding corporations had sold out. Fill the stores with cheap goods, sell at unjustifiably high prices, and the public be damned, they seemed to be saying. The companies had lost their Corporate Souls. The old operative words, like loyalty, service, quality, fairness, that previously defined the business were out. The merchants of avarice and greed focused on the current quarter's bottom line, to the exclusion of everything else. Nothing mattered anymore, but increased quarterly profits – every quarter, at any cost – as if *infinite* quarterly profit increases were actually *achievable*.

As I reflected on our conversation, later, I became aware of what I perceive to be parallels between the secular world and the Church. The parallels, as I see them, had their origins in the same approximate period in time, the 1960's and 1970's.

In the sixties, we experienced the emergence of various "ANTI" movements, such as the "Anti-War" movement,

147

which gave rise to other movements, such as the "Anti-Nuke" movement. I propose that the same forces were behind these so-called "movements". I propose, also, that these movements were harbingers of worse things to come. A process of polarization emerged and grew exponentially.

An ever increasing disrespect for traditional morals and values led, swiftly, to such National Cancers as the so-called "Free Love" movement and the illicit drug culture. Enormous damage was done to our American society, with astonishing speed. Herpes and Aids as well as certain other sexually transmitted diseases served to put a damper – to a limited extent – on the Free Love movement's so-called Sexual Revolution, but not before the tragic consequences of those diseases became a world-wide crisis that persists to this day.

The Drug Culture has not abated, but has become altered as the drug merchants of decline and death and the persistent *drug users* - After all, there can be no illegal, illicit drug problem, unless there are willing *Buyers*. –have found new ways to defeat the ever increasing efforts to enforce the law and put drug dealers out of business.

The Aids epidemic, initially almost entirely confined to male homosexuals, has now become a deadly health menace to men, women, and children throughout the world.

The parallels I see between the malaise of the secular world and the decline in the Church, though certainly different in character, are as devastating to the Church as they are to the nation. The Church is clearly under attack *from within*, in the wake of the Vatican II disruption of time honored, centuries old, Traditions and Rites. Vatican II did more to destroy devotion, reverence and piety among the faithful than any other influence the Church has endured in, at least, the past two centuries – and probably more. Vatican II was an unequaled disaster for the Catholic Church throughout the world.

The Church, today, is riddled with cancerous, shadowy, counterfeit organizations that operate under the guise of *"opening* the Church to the world outside", while they work constantly to infiltrate the Church infrastructure and systematically dismantle the traditions and the values of Holy Mother Church, and secretly insert heretical, humanist practices in their place. Feminist, Socialist, Marxist, homosexual and anti-life ideologies and influences are what the spectacularly failed Vatican II have allowed into the Church with its bungling naiveté. Whether the Church hierarchy participating in the workings of Vatican II and beyond were deceived or were knowing – and willing – participants in the proceedings I open to speculation. No one, however, can deny the fact that we have lost astonishing numbers of Priests and Religious. We have, today, virtually no Religious Brothers and Nuns – those who devoted their lives to God and taught our children in Catholic schools all over America. They are gone. There are no longer enough Priests in America to staff the Churches. Are these coincidental developments? I do not believe that. And regular Church attendance, in the range of 75% of American Catholics before Vatican II, now is down to a shameful 25% according to many polls.

Parallels. The demise of our National morals and values in America is mirrored by the demise of morals and values among Catholics in America – and across the world. Both situations have the beginnings in the awful decades of the sixties and seventies. I propose to you that the parallels are not coincidence. I believe the same forces, the forces of Satan, are allied and working tirelessly to destroy America and to destroy the Church.

The most frightening aspect of all of this lies in the apathy and acceptance of so many of our numbers. To stand on the sideline, wring your hands, shake your head, and cluck your tongue will not do anything to save Our Nation or our Church. If enough of us do not step forward and do our duty, get actively involved, and fight with all that is in us to restore the morals and virtues of both Church and Nation, we will lose both.

If you are one of those people who do not believe in Satan's existence, you are, excuse me for saying so, a fool, and very vulnerable to his desire to destroy you.

What kind of world do you want to leave to your grandchildren? It is squarely up to you to create and preserve that world for them.

Katrina's Troubling Mixed Lessons

Donald J. Cole, September, 2005
Cypress, TX,

The forces of nature have put all of the people along the Gulf Coast and south Florida to the test in recent weeks. The response to the human and economic impacts has been a mixed bag of astounding proportions. On one hand, the outpouring of support and assistance to the storm's casualties has been enormous. Everyday American people have opened their homes, their hearts, and their pocketbooks to help in every conceivable way.

Yet, while the public reaction and response has been excellent —even heroic— the performance of government agencies and jurisdictions has been abominable. On almost every level there were failures; from the local and state government entities, on up the chain to the federal government and its massive array of departments and agencies. It would serve no worthwhile purpose in this space to harp on which government agency, or which politician failed worse than which other(s).

What is particularly troubling, though, in the wake of the enormous, wide spread impacts, is the partisan polarization that persists; the incredibly unfounded attacks on the President, and the blatant attempts to turn these awful products of the ravages of nature into totally unfounded racial issues. This poisonous climate of hatred and self interest at such a time, when our common good and common resolve to be united in purpose is put to the test and appears to be falling short, raises serious questions about what is wrong in America today.

In spite of the massive person to person outpouring of help and support, our political infrastructure has a death-grip on *polarization and gridlock* . That is very bad news. If the Parties and all of the organizations within those Parties, and the special interests that lobby the Parties cannot unite in this urgent hour and work together, then pray earnestly for God's Help. We're going to need it.

The Church Under Siege

Donald J. Cole,   August, 2005
Cypress, TX,

Recently, Pope Benedict XVI publicly lamented the dying Church in America and Europe.   What a stunning announcement from the Holy Father!   And, how appropriate, his comments were. Can anyone fail to see the awful truth of how the Church, our Church, is dying before our eyes? All over America and all over Europe, the Church is riddled with groups and movements that are dedicated overturning everything we hold sacred.
One such organization is *"Call to Action"*. This group, which claims to be Catholic, will have their Annual National Conference in Milwaukee, WI this November 3-7.   Check out some of the highlights **(?)** of their program:

*"**Father**"* Richard McBrien will give his plenary speech entitled, "The Pontificate of Benedict XVI: A preliminary Assessment". Many American Catholics had the misfortune of seeing McBrien give his ***stammering*** "preliminary assessment" on TV when Pope Benedict was elected.

How about some of the other ***nonsensical*** presentations planned for the Conference:

Someone named Joy Barnes will present: "Personal to Political: How Women's Ordination Impacts the Global

Community". She crows that **women's ordination is solely a U.S. women's rights issue.**

And how about Lalor Cadley's "Mary Our Sister: Friend of God and Prophet"? Cadley leads *prayer with images, poetry, and music.* "Thanks to the revelations of Elizabeth Johnson and other Feminist Theologians, Mary of Nazareth, Jewish Peasant woman of faith, has been **released from her role as submissive handmaiden** and restored to her place as a powerful, prophetic woman".

Excuse me? Can you believe such basket cases as these can actually be given a forum?

Carolyn Gantner will lead morning *prayer of* **gentle Yoga and pranayama breathing.** "Yoga is a **sacrament,** *a* **symphony of souls and motion** . . . We bless the new day through sun salutation, half moon, mountain, and other yoga positions."

Understand . . . these nit-wits are representing themselves to be **Catholics!**

Joseph Kilikevice, OP, will lead the *Dances of Universal Peace as prayer in movement.* "We call upon God in ways that honor a rich diversity of traditions: Jewish, Christian, Muslim and others. Simple chants and reverent movement in a circle, open us to peace, reconciliation and solidarity with all people of the world". Interesting, huh?

And this guy is alleged to be an ordained Priest! How sad that our beloved Church is infested with the likes of these Mis-fits. Sounds like a very traditional Catholic program, doesn't it?

No? Well then you had better wake up to the fact that our American Roman Catholic Church is heavily infiltrated by groups and organizations like CTA who want to take the Church away from you and me.

The Subject Is Diversity

Donald J. Cole, JUNE, 2005
Cypress, TX

Diversity.

Can there be any word in today's world that is used more than this single word? The Random House Dictionary of the English language defines Diversity thus: Noun. 1. The state or fact of being diverse; difference; unlikeness. 2. Variety; Multiformity. 3. a point of difference

Now, the next word listed on page 388 of the random house dictionary, right below diversity, is the word *divert.*

Divert. defined as: 1. To turn aside or from a path or course; deflect. 2. To draw off to a different course, purpose, etc. 3. To distract from serious occupation; amuse.

I know a little bit about diversity. Ii was born and raised in New York City, you know – The Big Apple, formerly known as the great melting pot. But the great melting pot was not confined to the boundaries of the city of New York. The great melting pot was, more precisely, America.

In present day usage, the word *diversity* is applied incorrectly and has taken on a mantle of political correctness of astonishing proportions. the way that some politicians, corporate top managements, and those below them on the totem pole rhapsodize over the magical, mystical notion of *diversity* sometimes gives the appearance that those folks are in the throes of a deep religious experience.

What does the champion buzzword of twenty first century planet earth have to do with the great melting pot? The answer to that question is one simple word – *nothing.*

So where am I going with all of this? I will tell you as clearly and as plainly as I can. I submit to you all that this present day worship of the concept of so-called *diversity* is pure bunk. It is nonsense.

Let's get back to the melting pot of bygone days in early America. the melting pot was not a buzzword or a Cocktail Party catch phrase. The melting pot was a powerful engine of change; of motivation; of growth in all levels of our society; and of staggering positive accomplishment.

I have heard prominent individuals in business and politics, and everyday people on the street, toss off and demean the melting pot character of nineteenth and twentieth century America as an old outdated scheme

158

unworthy of the brilliant thinkers, movers and shakers of present day America. I hasten to point out here that though I am using America as my point of reference, I am well aware of the fact that the **diversity** wave is an international **tsunami**. And, I believe, there is great potential destructive force in that wave.

The American melting pot was, I propose to you, the single most important factor in the nation's ascendency to greatness in the world community. People came to America from every part of the globe, eager to jump into that marvelous melting pot and become a part of something greater than they had ever seen or even dared to dream of. All four of my own grandparents were part of that flood of humanity that came here and took their place in the great melting pot.

There are some people today who mistakenly believe that the melting pot resulted in "sameness" and that the melting pot idea was applied in American business for too long; that a better idea is that of a basket that weaves all of us as we are, together for a common purpose in business, but lets us contribute to that purpose while still being ourselves.

As one great thinker, who came before me once said: "poppycock"!

The true beauty and greatness of the melting pot was not that people of all kinds of diverse cultures and backgrounds all melted down to being the same. That is simply not true. Our nation represented something better for people of every race and ethnicity and they came together to become part of something new and original and better.

And in doing so, aware of and proud of their own individual heritage and ancestries, they **did not** focus their attention on their **differentness**. Instead they committed themselves to the concept – no, the virtue – of **Unity.**

Unity is what causes success in all worthwhile endeavors, not the **diversity** that is spouted everywhere today.

Unity is what is most lacking in this nation and in the world today. Unity is what will be the key to solving the enormous crises we face all over the world today – and nowhere worse -than here on our own soil.

I am only a second generation American. But I am as devoted to the principles that ushered this country onto the world stage and made us a great nation as any American. And I say to you that our drift away from that once **potent unity** has harmed us all. If America fails and sinks to the depths, the whole world will sink.
Now, I have to say it: it is time to turn away from the **perversity of diversity** and rediscover the luster of **unity**.

160

I thank the diverse legions of people who concentrated on building the uniqueness of the America I have known with its myriad of essences and flavors from all of the diverse corners of the world.

God Bless America . . . For What?

Donald J. Cole, March 24, 2005
Cypress, TX

It was the first Far East deployment for the "New" U.S.S. Yorktown CVA 10, following her 1952 re-commissioning at the Bremerton, Washington Naval Shipyard. As a young Navy Airman, attending my first "Moral Guidance" Lecture by the Catholic Chaplain, Father Ward, in Ready Room 2, a day or two before our scheduled arrival in Yokosuka, Japan, I was stunned when Chaplain Ward spoke those bitter words.

The good Padre was speaking out of frustration and dismay. He'd been around a long time and knew that his counsel against sexual promiscuity would go unheeded by most who heard it. His follow-up question was: "Why should God bless America, when so many Americans behave so sinfully?" I was offended those many years ago by his words.

Today, in light of the grotesque abuses of Terri Schindler Schiavo's constitutional right to "Life, Liberty, and the Pursuit of Happiness", I echo the stinging words of Chaplain Ward . . . God Bless America . . . **For** What ?

Should God bless our Nation for having sunk to such depths of depravity that we now join the likes of WWII Germany, Communist China, the Post WWII Soviet Union, and a host of other degenerate Nations and entities who embrace, or did embrace the hideous Culture of Death that is gradually (though ever increasingly) moving the world toward its ultimate destruction ?

How has America; founded as a God fearing, God loving bastion of freedom. Justice, respect, and morality, descended into the present day slime in which we now exist ? It did not happen overnight. The process began long ago. In retrospect, I have come to believe that Chaplain Ward was a Prophet. He stood in the vanguard of the small numbers of people who were then sounding the alarm that Americans were moving in the wrong direction and flaunting the blessings God had showered upon us.

Today, in America, there are mounting reflections of Adolph Hitler, Joseph Stalin, Mao Tse Tung, and their ilk in every corner of our government institutions. Our Congress, our Judiciary, State governments, Regional governments, Local governments, our Schools and

Universities, and sadly, even our Religious Institutions; all have been penetrated by God hating, America hating practitioners of the Culture of Death and Perversion.

Look around you ! Who among us is not capable of seeing and hearing the enormous body of evidence of America's (and, more importantly - Americans') decline into this tragic abyss of evil ?

In THIS WEEK ALONE, as I write this essay on March 24, 2005, look at a sampling of just a few of the current events in the news around our nation:

- Terri Schindler Schiavo's life is draining out of her, as she is being starved and dehydrated to death *by Court Order,* despite the absence of

- any documentary evidence of her consent to such treatment; and in the presence of a significant and growing body of circumstantial evidence of physical and psychological abuse that may have caused or contributed to Terri's condition, as well as extensive medical testimony that Terri is not (as ONE doctor declared on the basis of a forty-five minute examination, without using any more scientific assessment instruments than a *set of keys on a chain*) in a persistent vegetative state. Numerous doctors and other medical professional with extensive knowledge of and involvement in Terri's treatment over many years have repeatedly stated in public and in sworn affidavits filed with the renegade courts theta Terri is treatable and, with the proper therapy and treatment could substantially recover from her brain injury.
- A nine year old missing Florida girl's body is found, and a depraved, previously convicted sexual predator, who was not only no longer in prison, but was working in a school, confesses

- to her sexual assault and brutal murder. This case being but the latest in a continuing and increasing string of such evil crimes.

- In Minnesota, a sixteen year old boy with a history of disturbing behavioral problems and numerous traumatic family events (his father's suicide; his mother's severe brain injury from an auto accident) goes on a killing rampage at his home and school, killing nine people, including his own grandfather.

- In California, the trial of Michael Jackson for sexual abuse of a child continues. Jackson, the so-called pop-star entertainer, with a history of multiple past incidents charging him with sexual child abuses - and multi-million dollar payoffs to get the accusers not to pursue or cooperate in any criminal charges against him, nonetheless continues to have a sizeable retinue of apologists and supporters.

- Also in California, specifically in San Francisco, because the players have transformed the after game handshake tradition into a violent exercise of slapping and smacking each other around and verbally trashing each other, all after game contact is now banned . . . in the *Girls' Soccer League.*

- In Texas, the Texas Court of Criminal Appeals granted an eleventh hour stay of execution for a convicted murderer who, *fourteen years ago,* wantonly murdered an innocent storekeeper.

The killer's lawyer claims that the jury instructions for the murderer's sentencing were inadequate.

- The U. S. Supreme Court refused to hear the Terri Schindler Schiavo case, in a one page announcement that gave no reason or , or any information concerning the breakdown of the vote.
- . . . and these are but a sampling of this current week's tragic events.

How much evidence will it take to awaken the populace to the fact that our Nation; the precious gift of our Founders to us, purchased with their blood, sweat, and righteous determination, is starting to crumble. Never in our entire history have there been so many things wrong at one time. We have become fat, lazy, self-indulgent, and disconnected – from each other, and from our roots.

We are a house divided – and all who have the capacity to think, should know that a house Divided against itself, cannot stand.

When Abraham Lincoln spoke those words in the opening of his speech to the 1,000 delegates to the Illinois State Republican Convention on June 16, 1858 he was, of course, paraphrasing the words of Jesus Christ in the New Testament of the Holy Bible. The choice of words was unpopular with many, including some of Lincoln's friends and allies. But Lincoln said he wanted to use a *universally known figure of speech* that would rouse the people to the real peril of the times. [

Is there some irony here ? Would that phrase from the Bible – that Lincoln then considered to be universally known by the people - be *universally known* today ? I think, perhaps not]

Nor did Lincoln leave it at that universally known phrase. That was his call to attention. He followed that phrase by saying: "I believe this government cannot endure, permanently half slave and half free. I do not expect the Union to be dissolved – I do not expect the house to fall – but I do expect it will cease to be divided. It will become all one thing or all the other."

Mr. Lincoln closed his speech on that occasion with these words: "The result is not doubtful. We shall not fail – if we stand firm, we shall not fail. Wise counsels may accelerate, or mistakes delay it, but sooner or later, the victory is sure to come." That was America in 1858 – an America whose overwhelming majority of citizens remained steadfast in their belief and trust in God's Divine Providence. Mr. Lincoln's speech was given at a historic moment in time when the country was at the threshold of a crossroads. In the war between the states that followed, the Union did *stand firm.* And the victory was indeed won at an enormous cost of blood, sweat and tears.

Today, on March 24, 2005, Holy Thursday, I declare to you my fellow Americans; family, friends, and enemies alike: We are again a House Divide, though I tend to think it more accurate, perhaps, to say we are a House *Still* Divided.

Once more we face a crossroads. Once again we must stand firm, and defend the Union. "Defend the Union against what?" some might ask.

Election Reflections

Donald J. Cole, 2004
Cypress, TX

In the 1980's "Looking For Love In All The Wrong Places" was a popular country song. Recently, in the midst of a spirited political discussion among like-minded friends, that song title came to mind. The discussion focused on the perils of the present day mess the election process has become. It occurred to me that, collectively, we sounded like the singer lamenting, in song, his wrongheaded approach to finding love.

I can remember similar discussions as long as forty years ago. The subject in those days often was how to cure voter apathy. My position on that subject is much the same today as it was then. As an election judge, at the time, I was very pleased on one occasion when a voter in my precinct brought two visiting relatives with him to the polls and asked me to describe our election process to them. The relatives were visiting from Australia. We had a nice visit. They learned how our election process worked and I learned from them that, in Australia, every eligible voter is required to vote or face serious consequences that could be in the form of stiff fines or even jail time. I believe we should have similar requirements in America. My position on that issue has been the source of many a heated discussion with my Republican colleagues from those long ago days until this moment. I will explain my reasoning.

Let me preface my explanation with this clarifying statement. When I embraced the concept used in Australia, forty odd years ago, we did not have, in this great country of ours, the extensive array of corruptions in our election process that we have today. That said, it is important that you understand that my position on the Australian method does not extend to the many other major ills of our election process. I will address those other issues separately.

Here is my reasoning for the Australian idea. I believe that the single most important problem we must solve in America is that we do not have the representative government . . . "of the people, by the people, for the people" that the founding fathers initially crafted.

What we actually have today; what has evolved, or perhaps I should say "devolved", is purely and simply "Special Interest Government". Voter apathy, lack of participation in the process by all eligible citizens is the cause of the Special Interest Government effect. Voting is a privilege that ranks very high in the long list of privileges we enjoy in America.

No other people on earth, in the entire history of the world, enjoy the enormous list of privileges we have in our nation. In spite of that fact, perhaps because of it, many Americans, far too many, take our privileges for granted. That's a mistake that can have devastating consequences.

There is a flip side to privileges. Every privilege carries a price. The price of privilege is a complementary and equal degree of responsibility. When people fail or refuse to shoulder their fair share of responsibility, the privilege itself becomes tainted. At some point, the privilege might even be lost.

Today I hear some of the same objections about requiring every eligible voter to vote as I heard forty years ago: some of these people are too ignorant to vote; they don't understand the issues; they don't have the mental capacity to study the issues, and on and on it goes. I do not disagree with the folks who say there are some people among us who don't know – or care – what the issues are. But I believe those people, at least many if not most of them, could be educated. They could learn how to evaluate candidates and issues well

enough to vote for the people and issues they believe would be best for America, for themselves, and their families. I also believe, very strongly, that there are numerous ways to accomplish the education of those people. I will have more to say on that issue later on.

As things now exist in our election process, approximately fifty percent of citizens eligible to register to vote do not bother to register. Many of those people do not register because they believe that their single vote cannot make any difference. Others are content to go with the flow and take what comes. The bottom line is that approximately fifty percent of eligible voters are registered. Of the total number of registered voters, in a major election, like a presidential election, a sixty or seventy percent turnout of registered voters is considered outstanding. In lesser elections the turnout might be as low as ten percent or less of registered voters. This is a problem of astonishing proportions.

If, in a presidential election, there is a seventy percent turnout, then anything in excess of thirty- five percent of registered voters will decide that election. Looking closer, approximately seventeen and a half percent (17 ½%) of the total number of people eligible to vote will have decided the election. But there is worse news. In elections for state offices, county and local elections, propositions and bond elections, where 10 percent turnouts are not particularly uncommon, slightly more than five percent (5%) of those who are eligible to vote can decide those contests and issues.

Think of that! A little more than five percent of the people who are eligible to vote could, and often do decide the fate of important propositions that carry long term major tax consequences, choose who will fill local, county, or state offices that will decide many issues that could reach into your private life and property. If all of the above does not constitute a crisis situation, then someone will have to redefine the word crisis for me. It is a crisis, a growing crisis. And the crisis has put special interest groups in charge of your life. The crisis and the power of the special interests will continue to grow until either the people wake up and take action to reverse the trend or our country becomes the latest addition to the ash heap of failed societies that have piled up throughout the world's history.

The best way to ensure that we have representative government is to have every person who is eligible to vote registered and voting in every election. I am not a

Utopian, so I know that we could never achieve full participation. I know also that there must be a learning process to accompany any serious attempt to accomplish substantially full participation in the election process.

What I do not accept is the often heard argument that some people are "too stupid", "too uninformed", or "otherwise unfit" to vote. But keep in mind that the operative word is "eligible". The process of changing to a requirement that every "eligible" voter must vote would certainly involve revisiting and revamping the parameters that define eligibility. In the early days of our Republic, one had to be a *property owner to be eligible to vote. For many decades, women were not eligible to vote.*

The issue of an individual's fitness to be eligible to vote is a legitimate point for discussion and definition. But the discussion and defining, in order to be true to the concept of government "of the people, by the people, for the people", must be conducted of, by, and for the people – all of the people.

Our present day registration system is fraught with peril and wracked with abuses. Dead people shouldn't be voting. Convicted felons, incarcerated in prisons, should not be voting. Illegal aliens should not be voting. No person should have more than one current voter registration card, or find it possible in any way to cast more than a single vote in any election.

Yet every one of those conditions exists today in our system, and in alarming numbers in some areas. Whether or not we adopt a policy requiring all eligible citizens to vote, our election process and especially our registration process is compromised and absolutely must be repaired.

Allow me to go back to the song title that came to my mind in the discussion I mentioned in the opening paragraph: "Looking For Love In All The Wrong Places". It appears to me that we in 2004 America are "Looking For Solutions In All The Wrong Places". Even worse, we are collectively closing our eyes to many of the problems themselves; never mind how to solve them. I am being a bit facetious here, but in addition to the song reminder, I also recall a cartoon I saw many years ago. The 'toon depicted a large group of ostriches scattered around a field. All but one of them had his/her head buried in the sand. The one ostrich had his head up, looking around. The caption read: "Where'd everybody go?" Can you see a parallel anywhere in all of this?

I contend that massive election reform, from the registration process all the way through the campaigning and election process, is urgently needed in America, and soon. I offer the following to stimulate thought, discussion, and action. We all must carry our weight in the management of our Republic – that's the "by the people" part of the system. And it's a "use it or lose it" challenge.

Consider:

We have allowed the registration process to become polluted to the point of stinking. There is no excuse and no justification for the present mess. There is a commonly used expression in environmental contaminated site remediation circles that goes, "the solution to pollution is dilution". There, do you see how simple that is? What we must do to solve the problem of our severely polluted voter registration system is dilute the toxic constituents from the process until the process is purified. Friends, that is not difficult to do.

The first action should be to declare a National Voter Registration Period, say a three or four month window, during which every voter in every State is required to register anew, under specific new minimum guidelines that, once met, would permit any voter of any State under the new system, to vote in any National election. The primary requirement for every citizen to obtain registration would be to appear in person before a registration board official and show documentary proof of United States citizenship. Failure to provide the required documentary proof of U.S. citizenship would render the individual Ineligible to register to vote, until such time that the individual was able to present, in person, the required proof to the registration board.

In the case of sick, elderly, or otherwise handicapped individuals who would be unable to personally appear at the Registration board, accommodations would be available to those individuals to have a registration official visit such individuals at their place of residence. Other accommodations would be employed to make in person registration available to Ex-patriot Americans working abroad, Diplomats, Military personnel and such other U.S. citizens working and stationed outside of the United States.

Looking back to the discussion above concerning any refinements in defining the parameters for "eligibility", those components would also be part of the new registration process. With respect to local and state elections, each of the States could impose additional criteria for its registered voter citizens to establish and/or maintain eligibility to vote in State elections or local elections within the State. No voter in any State would be permitted to vote in any State or local election without having obtained National Voter Registration by satisfying the requirements to establish eligibility and proof us U.S. Citizenship.

Outline of the process for total reform.

The elements of the process to reform and repair the system of elections in America must be all inclusive including every aspect of the system from the registration process, through all of the campaigning components, also including the impacts to the system of practices and activities from any quarter of the public and private sectors, and through the actual election itself. Here are two outline roadmaps for the Reform Process

Outline One includes elimination of the "Party Process".

A number of the founding fathers, George Washington and John Adams among them, opposed the party system, believing it would have a divisive effect. The extreme polarization of the two major parties today ,

The Republican Party and the Democrat Party, gives weight to President Washington's and President Adams' belief.

<u>Outline Roadmap One</u>

<u>Political Parties</u>

With the Republican and the Democrat Party being the two major political parties in America, many people in our society refer tp our system as a "Two Party System". That, of course, is not an accurate statement. The existence of other minor parties, though it is played down in most quarters, can be a major influence in the outcome of an election.

Elections in recent history have shown that to be true, when a minor party candidate siphons off enough votes from one of the major party candidates to cause that candidate to lose the election to the other major party candidate. Generally, a substantial minor party candidate will take a significant number of votes away from only one of the major party candidates.

The likelihood of a minor party candidate actually winning an election is quite remote. In practice, minor party candidates, campaign rhetoric aside; usually fill the role of spoiler to one of the major party candidates.

Nevertheless, these minor parties that spring up from time to time usually only to disappear in a few years, consume just as the two major parties do, substantial amounts of resources – time and money. urces, the precious components that drive the engines of progress and prosperity, come in many varieties. There is an extraordinary array of natural resources, some finite, some renewable. Man-made resources, everything from refined products, such as oil and gasoline, steel, textiles, food products, pharmaceuticals, time and money are also part of the total range of resources.

In order to protect and preserve our American way of life and our world leadership position, we must use all of our resources wisely. I contend that for far too long, we have squandered resources in ever- increasing amounts on the party system of electing and managing our government. Allow me to illustrate:

Hundreds of millions of dollars, and millions of man-hours are expended in every election cycle to do nothing more than support the party process. Not one cent of those dollars, or one minute of those hours does anything to increase our Gross Domestic Product or improve our balance of trade with the world. Instead, the party system continues to grow and use up more and more resources that we would be far better off using to produce goods and services to be sold in the marketplace for profit.

Consider with me for a moment the powerful positive impact on our national economy and standard of living if those hundreds of millions were put to better, productive use. I mentioned textiles above among the man made resources we use. Think about the number of textile mills that have closed in America in the last couple of decades, replaced by mills in foreign countries. Think about the thousands of jobs that Americans lost in that process to lower paid foreign workers. Now reflect on how different the picture would be if, instead of pouring hundreds of millions into the proliferation of political party waste, those millions had been spent on U. S. textile products and wages for the American workers who made them and the salesmen who sold them to Americans at higher prices than imported goods.

Now spend a little time with your own imagination and see how many scenarios you can develop to illustrate how much better the enormous use of resources, time and money, currently wasted on perpetuating the party system, could be invested in America's productivity.

The party system is an increasing drain on our resources and growing cancer on our election process. The party system has degenerated to the point that we have toxic polarization with obscene amounts of time, money, and resources feeding both sides. The time has come to recognize the wisdom of those founders like Washington, Adams and others of their contemporaries who counseled against such a system. We need to get back to our roots, to our fundamental founding values. The party system must end.

The New Process:

- Dismantle all political parties.
- All candidates for election run independently with no "Party" organization affiliation.
- Each candidate is allowed to establish a campaign committee or organization to develop strategies and manage the candidate's campaign. The campaign organizations may be organized and commence operations three

179

months in advance of the primary day voting and may continue operations within established guidelines (TBD) for as long as the candidate remains as an active candidate and, if elected on election day, for a period of one month after election day.

- As many eligible candidates who wish to run for an office may do so. There is no limit on the number of eligible candidates who may present themselves for an office to run for that office in the primary day voting.
- The two candidates who receive the highest number of votes on primary day will be certified
- as the two candidates who will run for the office on Election Day.
- The Electoral College will remain in place in presidential elections and will function as it does today. As is done today, the Electoral College will convene, after the election, and electors from every state will cast their votes for the winning candidate from their respective states.
- State and local primaries and elections for all offices will be conducted in the same manner as described above.
- Initiatives, Propositions, Bond Elections and all such similar matters will appear on the ballot on Election Day as they do now.

Term Limits:

Any program for election reform should include provision for discussion of term limits. Term limits for State offices, and for local offices within a particular state, must be determined solely by the voters of the particular state. However, term limits for all National offices, President/Vice President, United States Senators, and Congressmen, could – and I believe should – be part of the election reform, with the stated provision that all states would, at their own option, subsequently have the right to enact, or not enact, term limits by means of whatever method the particular state might choose to employ.

Polling:

No polling concerning any election for National office will be permitted by any organization for any purpose. Polling has become a major part of the pollution of the election process in America.

Polling organizations, large and small, can and sometimes do conduct polls for the sole purpose of creating, rather than measuring trends and opinions. Polling, it may be argued, provides allegedly valuable information to candidates and Parties about any number of conditions. It is probably true that polling could provide such benefits to parties and/or candidates.

But the record over the years since polling has become such a large component of what is today's election process shows that there are far too many opportunities to create detrimental impacts on the election process and, in some cases, the outcome of certain elections.

I contend that polling provides no true benefit to anyone but special interests, be they political organizations, industry organizations, labor organizations, media outlets and others, but no true benefit to the voters of this Nation.

Polling can rightfully be included in any list of detrimental practices that have contributed to the pollution of the election process. As such, it should be banned from the process entirely.

An Appeal to Reason and Logic

Donald J. Cole, September, 2003
Cypress, TX

On Saturday, September 13, 2003, we have an election in Texas to decide on twenty-two proposed Constitutional Amendments.

The Amendments cover a wide range of issues, some more important than others. Here is a thumbnail summary of the issues covered:

Veteran's land funds; Mineral interests; Religious property tax exemptions; Utility District Parks; Travel trailer tax exemption; Home equity reverse mortgages; Reducing certain juries to six; Canceling certain elections; Public Schools endowment fund investments; Donating used fire-fighting equipment; Texas wineries wine sales; Allowing the legislature to set maximum amounts for pain and suffering in lawsuits; Extending over 65-school tax freeze to city, county and other property taxes; Allowing TxDot to borrow short-term funds; Preventing cities/counties reducing employee retirement;

Allowing Home Equity lines of credit; Extending disabled property taxes; Prohibiting new rural fire prevention districts; Improvement Bonds cites w/ military bases; Allowing Public University professors to be paid for service on water boards; Filling a temporary vacancy, when elected official called to military service.

I urge you to get copies of these Proposed Amendments, study them and the Non-Partisan analyses of them and vote, after thoughtful consideration. If you will not take the time to study and reflect on the proposed Amendments, I urge you to stay home and do no harm to our State Constitution.

My primary reason for writing to you is to urge you to **VOTE NO on Proposition 12**.

- Proposition 12 is a really BAD idea that will HURT Texas families who have already been hurt.

- Proposition 12 will not reduce Doctors' Malpractice insurance premiums.

- We need MEDICAL QUALITY REFORM and INSURANCE REFORM first, then Tort Reform

- Voluntarily surrendering your Constitutional rights to Politicians, Insurance companies and other wealthy special interests is sheer madness.

- Ask yourself if a Loved one's life would be worth more than $250,000 if a *BAD DOCTOR* killed him/her. Proposition 12 says **no life is worth more under any circumstances.**

- There are more booby traps in Prop 12, too, in the "other Actions" portion (beginning in 2005).

184

Look at some of the backers of Prop 12...they are a collection of big lobbying organizations who represent Insurance and Pharmaceutical Companies, Big Construction, Chemical, and Oil & Gas Companies, For-profit Nursing Home Operators and others. These organizations masquerade as public interest or grass roots organizations who represent your interest. They Do Not!

I am a lifelong Republican Conservative...and I am NOT about to surrender my Constitutional rights to a bunch of untrustworthy politicians, insurance companies and other special interests who are already bleeding us dry. <u>GIVE UP RIGHTS FOR PROTECTION BY POLITICIANS?</u> Can anyone truly think that's good?

NOT ME...NOT NOW...NOT EVER.

Do We Need Nature?

Donald J. Cole, August 2003
Cypress, TX

The competition[1] question, "Do We Need Nature?" at first glance seemed absurd. Surely, no thinking person could believe that we do not "need" Nature. All things exist within the essence of Nature. Humankind, the animal kingdom, the plant world, the mineral resources of the universe, religions, the sciences, and the philosophies, everything in the universe exists within the framework of Nature. We are part of Nature. Thus, it appears obvious that we "need Nature".

One is tempted to say, in reply to the question, "Define Nature". The Random House Dictionary of the English Language defines the word "Nature" as follows:

1.The particular combination of qualities belonging to a person, animal, thing, or class by birth, origin, or constitution. 2. the instincts or inherent tendencies directing conduct. 3. character, kind, or sort: two recent books of the same nature. 4. the material world, esp. that part unaffected by man. 5. plants, animals, geographical features, etc., or the places where these exist largely free of human influence. 6. the universe, with all its phenomena. 7. the sum total of the forces at work throughout the universe. 8. the true appearance of anything: a portrait true to nature.

9. the biological functions or the urges to satisfy their requirements. 10. the laws and principals believed to be followed naturally and rightly by living beings: an act that is against nature. 11. the original, natural, uncivilized condition of man. 12. a primitive, wild condition; an uncultivated state. 13. by nature, as a result of inherent qualities; innately.

In this age of ever accelerating, rates of change, new discoveries and evolving scientific development, the definition of the word "Nature" expands to accommodate new discoveries, refinements, and altered perspectives. Therefore, the essay question, "Do We Need Nature?" begs an answer from a specific perspective, or perspectives.

Every living being has some perception of what "nature" is. Obviously, though we humans can observe animal behaviors and come to some conclusions on how some animals appear to perceive "nature", unfortunately those living creatures cannot add anything to the dialog in any assessment of whether or not we need nature. The existence of these animals, however, bears on the manner in which humans make their own individual assessments of whether, or how much, or how little we need nature.

This essay examines present day political, societal and scientific characteristics, measured against the above definition of the word "nature"; and answers the question, "Do We Need Nature", within the framework of the definition, from the perspective of a second generation American Christian of Irish descent.

Applicable requirements for length preclude an exhaustive analysis here of all of the elements and issues the question raises. However, an answer, from the declared perspective is presented here in full.

"It's the nature of the beast" is a phrase commonly used to emphasize that certain people, things and even situations carry in them a particular combination of qualities or characteristics which make them recognizable, as referenced in part 1 of the definition above. Absent some of those particular qualities, the combination then becomes unfamiliar and the person, thing, or situation displays a different nature; appears unnatural.

When faced with someone or something that appears out of the normal range most people approach and interact with that person or thing in a manner that is out of the ordinary, unnatural. Follow a hypothetical encounter involving a person, thing or situation missing some or all of the particular qualities commonly seen in such a person, thing or situation and a person who displays a correspondingly different or unnatural response. The outcome of the encounter, the net result of the interaction, will invariably be much different than usual, out of the ordinary, unnatural. The unnatural response to unnatural circumstances described above illustrates the second part of the definition of Nature.

Part three of the definition exposes the basis for the "…nature of the beast" phrase.

Part four, "the material world, especially that part unaffected by man" is interesting because the part of the material world not affected by man is continually shrinking. Somehow, the notion seems to have grown disproportionately high that man affecting the material world is a negative condition. However, there can be no doubt that frequently when the material world is affected by man, the effects prove to be highly beneficial.

No reasonable case can be made to support a claim that man's actions or inactions never produce a negative effect on the material world. However, effects, be they good or bad must be measured by degrees. The degree of negative or positive outcome must be evaluated on the basis of what is favorable or unfavorable for the whole of "Nature". Risk is inherent in "Nature", in all of Nature. For example: childbirth, one of the most fundamental building blocks of nature, carries a significant degree of risk. Both the mother and the child are subject to multiple dangers through the birthing process.

We can manage the risk and reduce the degree of danger by applying the knowledge gained from scientific and technological research and development. Yet, even with all of the knowledge and technology at our disposal, we cannot remove all of the risk in the process.

Part 5, 6, 7, and 10, taken together constitute what many, probably most people, think of when they consider a definition of Nature. This is also the defined portion of Nature that produces the overwhelming majority of issues that relate directly to the question, "Do We Need Nature?" All manner of charges of real or imagined abuses of "Nature" are tossed about every day. Enormous amounts of time, effort, financial and other resources are consumed in the pursuit of actions claiming to have, as their aim, protection of Nature or The Environment. The remaining definition parts: numbers 8, 9, 11, 12, and 13 are peripheral to the question at hand.

The inescapable truth imbedded in the question, "Do We Need Nature?" is that we are "Nature". That is to say, we are an integral component part of the whole. We cannot decide that we need or do not need "Nature". Nature itself, in its total context dictates that.

We can decide for ourselves if we need certain species of animals. We have the power as well to decide whether or not use up or consume all of a particular natural resource, such as trees, for example. It goes without saying that if we opted to do so, there would be extremely negative impacts to the whole of nature that would create a wide range of unfavorable consequences in our daily lives. And when examined more closely, even though we as humans could make a personal decision that we should use up all of the earth's trees, the reality of the natural order is such that a one hundred percent consensus could never be reached. Thus the notion that; given the superior place in the natural order that we humans enjoy; Nature provides inherent safeguards against its own destruction, that would preclude such a notion from coming to fruition.

Despite the frequent, shrill calls to the contrary, the sky is not falling, after all. At the end of the day, every day, "Nature" has advanced yet a little further.

Do We Need Nature? Yes, we need Nature in the same way we need the blood that courses through our bodies and supports our lives. Without the blood, we cease, at least in the physical sense, to exist. And Nature needs us, in the same way. We are part of the whole of Nature. Our endeavors, though sometimes causing injury, intentional or not, to one or another part of Nature, nevertheless, advance the preservation of Nature overall.

Nature generates countless challenges and perils from within. The manner in which we human beings deal with those challenges and perils is, of course, of utmost importance.

The key to the survival, preservation, and advancement of Nature is balance; just as the key to maintaining a healthy body is a well-balanced diet and well-balanced physical activity.

To be sure we face many crucial areas of opportunity to extend certain areas within the whole of Nature. Just as surely, we are presented daily with dangerous opportunities, which if managed improperly or incorrectly, have the potential to seriously imperil the crucial balance of the natural order.

In dealing with all of the serious issues of danger and opportunity we face in the world, day by day, we must study very carefully Nature's own order and arrangements. In exploring ways to deal with issues such biodiversity, genetic alteration, cloning, gene research and treatment, we must look back as much as look forward. We must be ever vigilant to the true orders of the divisions of Nature and be good stewards of the creator's gifts. It is not man's place in Nature to supplant nature or natural processes. We are not Gods. We should not presume to create anything we might perceive to be better that that which the creator has made. Our efforts should be focused upon extending and refining the creator's handiwork, not replacing it.

All of Nature is the gift of the Creator. The gift is to be cherished and enjoyed, protected and Preserved. Those who would claim that Nature is not a creation, but rather an accident, surely, must never have seriously reflected upon the intense wonders of the order and balance of Nature, nor of the exquisite beauty and complexity of everything from the smallest insect or plant to the awesome and magnificent detail of the human being.

Yes, we need nature. We are nature. We must pursue its development with utmost respect for the natural order, weighing decisions that will have a significant impact upon Nature in the context of what is best for the whole of Nature and is not an affront to the Creator. There are those who will take actions that will harm Nature, with no sense of respect, responsibility or remorse for their actions. That there are such individuals is a part of the overall human condition – "the nature of the beast", so to speak. We must, by our own commitment, ensure that such individuals and attitudes never become the majority of our species.

The Flood Waters Are Rising

Donald J. Cole, 2003
Cypress, Texas

There is a story about a man who lived in a home that was inside the flood plain in the Metro Houston area

It seems there was a severe tropical storm that hit the area and residents were advised to evacuate their homes in the neighborhood where the gentleman lived. We will call the gentleman Mr.Waiting for reasons that will become obvious. As the storm grow stronger and dumped ever increasing amounts of rain on his neighborhood, the local sheriffs made the rounds of the neighborhood and urged the residents to evacuate the area. "No, said Mr. Waiting, I'll be fine. The Lord will take care of me." Time passed and the storm grew worse. The sheriffs again came through the area, and again urged Mr. Waiting to evacuate. "No, said Mr. waiting, as I told you before, the Lord will take care of me." The storm intensified and water began rising in the neighborhood. The water rose to a point that cars and trucks could no longer get the through the streets.

Then, a small boat made its way to the home of Mr. Waiting. There were several of Mr. Waiting's neighbors in the boat. All of them urged Mr. Waiting to leave his house and get to safety with them in the boat. "No,

194

thank you, said Mr. Waiting, there is no need. The Lord will take care of me." In time, the floodwaters had risen so high that Mr. Waiting had to move up to the second floor of his home. The entire first floor was underwater. As he stood by an open window on the second floor of his home, another large boat, this one from the Sheriff's Department, came up alongside the open window where Mr. Waiting stood looking out at the rising water. "Get into the boat, sir and we will get you to safety", said the deputy to Mr. Waiting. "Thank you Sheriff", said Mr. Waiting, " but that won't be necessary. The Lord will take care of me."

A couple of hours later, as it was growing dark, Mr. Waiting was forced by the rising water to climb up onto the roof of his submerged home. The situation was truly desperate. Then, swooping down from the eastern sky, a Coast Guard helicopter came alongside the home of Mr. Waiting hovered overhead. The crew lowered a large basket and called to Mr. Waiting over their PA system. "Climb into the basket, sir, and we will hoist you up into our helicopter and bring you to safety." "No, thank you very much, but that won't be necessary. You see", said Mr. Waiting, "the Lord will take care of me."

The crew of the helicopter pleaded over and over with Mr. Waiting to get into the basket so they could bring him to safety. But Mr. Waiting only repeated, again and again, that the Lord would take care of him. Late that night, as the floodwaters rose even higher, Mr. Waiting was swept away and drowned.

Then . . . Mr. Waiting found himself standing before what he realized where the gates of heaven.

Soon thereafter, St. Peter appeared at the gates. "Hello, Mr. Waiting", said St. Peter. "Hello? Is that all you have to say", said Mr. Waiting? "I placed all my trust in the Lord and he abandoned me. And all you have to say is hello?" St. Peter was quite disturbed by Mr. Waiting's outburst. "I don't understand", said St. Peter. "There must be some mistake. Please, give me a moment to look into this matter." While St. Peter was off checking on the details of this very troubling situation, Mr. Waiting stood around in front of the gates of heaven and grumbled continuously, to all who passed by, about the way that the Lord, whom he had trusted to take care of him, had, instead, abandoned him.

In a short time, St. Peter returned, holding a large bound volume. "There must be some mistake, some misunderstanding", said St. Peter. "I have checked thoroughly. The information I have here is that you were involved in a flood. According to my information, the Lord sent a sheriff's car twice, a neighbor's boat, a sheriff's launch, and a Coast Guard helicopter to take care of you and that you refused all of those offers of help."

It's interesting how we all fail to recognize situations that require us to take positive action. How easy it seems to just sit back and wait for the Lord to take care of all the problems we face. And then, when the Lord makes it clear to us what we need to do, we somehow do not get the message. I am sure that all of you like me have heard the expression: "God helps those who help themselves."

Now I would like to draw some parallels to the story I just related to you, because we are in the midst of a flood of a different kind. Some of us have been asking the Lord to take care of us, to rescue us from the flood that is growing and threatening to drown us. Consider some of the elements of this "flood" that threatens to destroy us today, this very moment.

Our church has been wracked with scandal about priests who have preyed upon young innocents, and committed vile acts of depravity, desecrating the priesthood and shaming the church. Certain of the hierarchy in the church have further disgraced the church by covering up the sinful, and criminal, acts.

There is a huge problem of homosexuals within the ranks of our clergy that goes on without any visible, significant challenge; with no real observable effort to cure and correct it.

Other churches, in the Protestant denominations, have similar problems. One Episcopal diocese has named an openly practicing, non-celibate homosexual as its bishop. Another Episcopal diocese, in Washington, DC, has a bishop who preaches that Scripture should be "massaged" to reflect modern attitudes, and also advocates ordaining non-celibate homosexual priests.

Three separate Councils of the Boy Scouts of America, long under siege by the forces that promote the homosexual agenda, the San Francisco, Boy Scout Council, a Massachusetts Boy Scout Council, and the Philadelphia, PA Boy Scout Council, have included "Sexual Preference" as one of the categories to be protected from discrimination in their organizations.

The United States Supreme Court, the same court that gave us the Roe-v- Wade decision that legitimized abortion 30 years, and nearly 40 million dead babies ago - think of that - 40 MILLION DEAD BABIES, killed in the name of "convenience"; that same Supreme Court has just recently struck down a Texas law against homosexual sodomy, trampling all over states rights in the process.

So where are my going with all of this? The fact is that dozens more issues could be included in this exercise. What we *can't seem to do anything about these problems*. We have to feed our families, get to bed and get some rest, go to our jobs tomorrow and do all of the STUFF we do; like playing golf, going fishing, playing with the kids, going to the movies, and all the other enrichment activities we get involved in. We go to church, and we pray - *a lot*. Well I, for one, do not buy that line.

When you put your head on the pillow tonight, remember what Mr. Waiting did about his problems - and make no mistake - the problems I pointed out here are your problems and mine. We, you and me, are the ones who have to deal with them and find solutions to them. So what will you do? What can you do?

Will you, for example, put pen to paper and write to your pastor, your bishop and every one of your government representatives and demand a return to the morality and decency that made our church and our nation the blazing beacons of faith and justice our church and our country were to the world?

The flame that illuminates those beacons is dimming dangerously low, and must be tended to. Will you stand, as a soldier of Christ, and do everything you can to restore the health of our church and our country? You can, if you choose to.

I expect we will see that helicopter hovering overhead before too much more time passes.

Patience And Prudence

Donald J. Cole, January 1, 2003

Cypress, TX

As we stand at the threshold of the New Year, I find myself considering the notion that, even though I don't usually make New Year's resolutions, it might be good to make an exception this year. But if I would do so, I thought, the resolutions I would make would have to be important and not numerous as to make achieving them unlikely.

After reflection, I decided that I would, indeed, make one resolution to pursue significant growth in my capacity of two virtues which I believe to be of great importance: Patience and Prudence.

To help me in my quest, I dug through some of my old resources to find inspiration that would help me stay on track. This is my personal resolution, which binds no one else. However, I commend this resolution to you for your consideration. I will keep close at hand the following words of wisdom, uttered by wise men and women, to help me stay the course.

ON PATIENCE . . . consider the following: Patience is not passive. On the contrary, it is concentrated strength. And also . . . There's no music in a "rest", but there's the making of music in it. And people are always missing that part of the life melody, always talking of perseverance, and courage, and fortitude. But Patience is the finest and worthiest part of fortitude, and the rarest, too. John Ruskin said that.

Decker said: Patience! Why it is the soul of peace; of all virtues it is the nearest kin to heaven; it makes men look like Gods. The best of men that ever wore earth about Him was a sufferer — a soft, meek, patient, humble, and tranquil spirit; the first true Gentleman that ever breathed.

And this, in Buffon's words: Never think that God's great delays are God's denials. Hold on. Hold fast. Hold out. Patience is genius.

Consider, also, the words of Laveter, who said: He surely is most in need of another's patience, who has none of his own. Sir Walter Scott cautioned: The sincere and earnest approach of the Christian to the throne of the Almighty, teaches the best lesson of patience under affliction, since wherefore should we mock the Deity with supplications, when we insult Him by murmuring under His decrees.

And lastly, on Patience, these words of W.S. Plumer: Be patient in little things. Learn to bear the everyday trials and annoyances of life quietly, calmly, and then, when unforeseen trouble or calamity comes, your strength will not forsake you.

ON PRUDENCE . . . Reflect on these words of Thomas a' Kempis: A prudent lover does not consider so much the gift of the lover, as the love of the giver.

It is noteworthy, in the words of S.G. Goodrich that: Aristotle is praised for naming Fortitude as the first of virtues. But he might, with propriety, have placed Prudence before it. Since, without Prudence, Fortitude is madness.

J. Mason's gift to us was these words: Prudence is a conformity to the rules of reason, truth, and decency, at all times, and in all circumstances. It differs from wisdom only in degree; wisdom being nothing but a more consummate habit of Prudence.

And lastly, these words of Mark Twain's; It is by the goodness of God that in our Country we have those three unspeakably precious things: Freedom of Speech, Freedom of Conscience, and the Prudence never to practice either.

My Most Memorable Christmas

Donald J. Cole, December, 2002
Cypress, TX

The year was 1953. I was an eighteen-year-old crewmember of the aircraft carrier USS Yorktown. We finished our rotation on the line off the coast of Korea and were fortunate enough to be heading to Hong Kong, instead of our usual overseas home port of Yokosuka, Japan. Hong Kong was a great Liberty port. Ask any U.S. Sailor. This time it was unique.

We learned, a couple of days before making port, that we would be hosting a Christmas party for a large group of Chinese orphan children. All of us crew members were enthusiastic about the idea of hosting this party for the kids. Few of us, though, were prepared for the stories of those kids we welcomed aboard and entertained, fed and gave gifts of the basic needs, like soap, washcloths, towels, toothbrushes and such; items that we all took for granted and would have never considered to be items to give as Christmas presents. But to those children, these articles were absolute luxuries.

We had the children aboard a couple of days before Christmas. They came to us from Kowloon, where an order of Catholic Nuns operated a home for orphans. Kowloon was off limits for us. We were not allowed to go there because it was under Communist Chinese control.

Each of us Sailors took one child under our care and gave them the grand tour of our huge ship. We took them all through the ship and finally, brought them up to the flight deck and sat each one of them in the cockpit of one of our jet aircraft. The children were thrilled by the experience and the attention we paid to them.

Most of us, that day, signed up to "adopt" one of the children for a year. That meant, simply, setting up a deduction of ten dollars per month from our pay to help support the child at the orphanage. My little girl was nine years old and had walked nearly eight hundred miles from deep inside mainland China, when her parents were both killed. I don't know whatever became of her. I have always prayed that she had a decent life.

On Christmas Eve, I was upset because I had drawn a work party that was to last all day. I, and several of my shipmates had an invitation to attend Christmas Eve dinner at the home of one of the U.S. consulate Attaches. I had hoped to go ashore and pick up some sort of gift for our hosts. That was not to be.

The working party was on the fantail (the aft end of the ship). I spent the entire day that Christmas Eve lowering garbage cans from our fantail down to the decks of small Sampans.

The Chinese on the Sampans would empty the contents of each garbage can onto their deck and begin sorting things out. Meat over here, green vegetables over there, breads over here and so on. The key to all of this was that "Mary Soo's Side Cleaners" had a contract to paint the entire hull of our nine hundred plus foot long ship. We furnished the paint. The contract price was ten dollars U.S. and all of our garbage while we were in port for a week or so.

I watched those people all day long as they sorted through our garbage and anticipated the wonderful meal they would make of our garbage.

How, I wondered, can such differences exist? Why do I have so much when these poor people have so little? All day, I lowered those garbage cans and learned a great lesson from those poorest of poor people. Later, my mates and I attended the dinner we'd been invited to and had a fine evening of good food and a taste of home, complete with Christmas carols around the piano and a beautifully decorated Christmas tree.

We returned to the ship in time for Midnight Mass on the hanger deck, which other work parties that day had decorated and transformed into a place that looked as if it had always been a Church. The beautiful Mass included music by our Choir and the ship's band.

That Christmas Eve work party brought into crystal clear focus for me the true meaning of a phrase I had heard from one of the Nuns who taught me in grammar school: Give yourself away . . . to those who need you.

Here's What I Think . .

Donald J. Cole, November 5, 2002
Cypress, TX

I have never been a Democrat, though I came from a family of democrats; never believed in the Democrat's "Party line". In the early years of our marriage, Patsy and I were "the Republicans" in our Brooklyn, NY Precinct. When we moved back to Texas in 1961, we were the "other Republicans" in our Corpus Christi precinct. Many of my good friends claimed to be "Conservative Democrats". In Time, they realized you couldn't be "Conservative" and Democrat. They became Republicans. Now, my "Moderate Democrat" friends have discovered they can't be "Moderate" and Democrat. San Francisco Ultra Left-Winger, Nancy Pelosi, will be Democrat Minority leader in the House.

This Pro Partial-Birth Abortion, Pro Homosexual rights, Anti American Values woman, who also calls herself a Catholic, and crows about her children and grandchildren will now lead the so-called Democrats. What a sham. There isn't any Democrat Party anymore. It's dead – by its own hand. What remains, slumped in the ashes is a rag tag collection of Communists, Socialists and America haters. Someone tell me, please. How can anyone be both Catholic and Democrat? How is that possible?

The Doctor is Out

Donald J. Cole, 9/2002
Cypress, TX,

Can you remember when doctors made House Calls? It always made more sense to me that a healthy doctor would visit a sick person's home to treat him or her. It seems backward that we do the opposite today. Sick people leave their homes, travel to the doctor's office and bring their illness with them to share with all the other waiting sick people and the healthy folks who transported them to the doctor's office.

It is a well established fact that things go in cycles. Could it be that we will see doctor's once again making house calls as they did before? My forecast is that it will happen sooner than many people think.

There are many doctors in America who are fed up with the rat race; the relentless pursuit of the almighty dollar that is so prevalent in the everyday routine of our times.

Already, there are scattered reports of doctors making house calls in small country towns. There seems to be a new breed of young doctors emerging who are more interested in healing the sick than living in high style in the big cities.

The stress and the risk associated with living in overcrowded cities figures in more and more decisions by people in all walks of life to do whatever they can to find a simpler, slower and more satisfying way to live with their families. The return to the practice of making House Calls does not, however, have to be limited to small rural areas. Doctors with practices whose patients are more or less concentrated in one or a few neighborhoods in the city may also find there is an up-side to making House Calls.

It certainly makes more sense from the sick patient's point of view. Also, the potential reduction of the spread of communicable disease could result in enormous savings in total treatment costs. Think of the possible trickle down benefits from that. As fewer patients become ill, fewer people require a doctor's care and medicine. Insurance costs would be reduced. Lower insurance premium costs would follow.

No, we won't see an overnight move toward the resumption of House Calls by doctors everywhere. But look for a return to the practice to come gradually, slowly at first, then pick up speed as more doctors see a way it can work for them.

You can help. Talk to you family and neighbors about the issue. Ask your doctor how he feels about house calls. Bring up the subject at church discussion groups. Promote the idea to everyone you know.

Our American Holocaust

Donald J. Cole, September, 2002
Cypress, TX

With great regularity, the world is reminded from many quarters about Adolf Hitler's World War II "Holocaust". The Nazi madman, Hitler, surely was one of the most charismatic murderers in the history of the world. He managed, somehow, to get his Generals to sign on to, their troops carry out, and most of the German people to endorse and support his grotesque plan to exterminate millions of human beings. Most, though not all, of the millions who died in the Holocaust were Jews.

Hitler hated Jews. Under the guise of what was good for the "Fatherland"; and under cover of wartime conditions, he convinced most Germans that Jews were somehow responsible for all of Germany's problems and were, thus, enemies of Germany. The German people, those who supported Hitler and those who did not, allowed Hitler's evil plan to continue until Germany was conquered by the Allied forces (America, notably, being the leading Nation of the forces that won the

victory over Germany). To the present day, and surely beyond today for all time to come, Germans bear the shame of Hitler's Holocaust . . . of Germany's Holocaust.

On January 22, 1973, a new Holocaust commenced . . . an American Holocaust . . . "Our American Holocaust". I call it "Our American Holocaust" because we, the people of America, have either endorsed, supported or, at the very least, have permitted this American disgrace to continue to this day nearly thirty years since its start.

On January 22, 1973, the Supreme Court of the United States, rendered its Decision in 410 U.S. 113, the case entitled Roe, et al V. Wade, District Attorney of Dallas County. That historic Decision was the act that enabled the commencement of Our American Holocaust. The carnage continues today all across our nation. More than thirty million innocent human beings have been put to death, exterminated, with the blessing of the United States government and the permission of the people of the United States. Thirty Million!

Yes, there are many who declare that they are "Pro-Life", yet they take no action to support their declaration or to defeat the killing. These are not evil people. However, their collective aversion to conflict, fear of being unpopular or being disliked; laziness; lack of commitment; or whatever it is that keeps them from actively participating in efforts to end the genocide of American Abortion . . . Our American Holocaust, makes them the same as the people of Hitler's Germany of World War II. Certainly no better, and probably much worse than those German people who were, after all, influenced by the tremendous disinformation from their

Fuhrer and his Chief henchmen and distracted by bombs falling around them.

Abortion in America today, right now, is being committed in the name of women's rights. That boils down, in a staggering majority of cases, to a woman's right to have an abortion as a means of contraception; to kill the baby she conceived in the course of her action borne of the desire for sexual pleasures. Numerous other choices for contraception could have been employed that would have prevented the creation of a human life. One can only conclude that millions of women (and men) engage in the pursuit of sexual gratification with total disregard for the potential consequences of their selfish desire and inexcusably reckless abandon.

These people are morally bankrupt and, with the added complication of various taxpayer funded government agencies footing the bill for the cost of committing millions of these abortions, Life, which is a gift from God, has been cheapened. People who engage in behavior that creates life, and then kill it, stain the fabric of America.

How Much Freedom Should We Trade For Our Security?

Donald J. Cole, August, 2002
Cypress, TX

SUMMARY

Freedom is the lifeblood of the human spirit. Throughout the entire span of the recorded history of humankind, Freedom stands alone as the most sought after condition of human existence. Freedom! It is the treasure of all treasures. Next to good health, freedom is the most vital element in building a constructive, meaningful, and rewarding life. The well-worn axiom, "Freedom isn't free", as cliché as it has become, never has been truer than it is today. In fact, it can be said To consider trading freedom for security is tantamount to giving away part of your most valuable asset in return for nothing at all. The core issue is that there can be no security without freedom. Security is contingent upon; depends upon freedom. In using or applying freedom, we *choose*, we act, or do not act upon whatever is at issue. But the *choosing*, in and of itself, is an *active* process that we *control*. The other side of the proposed exchange – security – is neither *active* nor do we *control* it. Security, at least a type of purported security that would require us to surrender any of our priceless freedom, is a bad investment.

In the final analysis, we should not be willing to trade *any* freedom for *any* security. Rather, we should intensify our pursuit of those who threaten our freedoms, find them and remove them. The only true security of any real value will be that which comes from eradicating the sources that threaten freedom.

Perhaps the thing about freedom that is most taken for granted, by the majority of people who enjoy its benefits, is that the very freedom they so enjoy and take for granted was a gift to them. The gift of freedom initially purchased over centuries of great sacrifice by millions who came before us carries with it no guarantee that it will endure. The preservation of freedom dictates that all who would keep it must pay the ongoing cost and must also purchase it for their children and their children's children who will come after them.

On a clear day bathed in bright sunshine, a meadow near Windsor, England, known as Runnymede, became famous in May of the year 1215 as the site of the signing of the Magna Charta by King John of England. Though it may not have been primarily intended as an instrument to grant freedom or individual human rights to the common people, the document, in large measure, did have the effect of doing so to a great extent. In the long haul, the Magna Charta enabled people who had never tasted freedom to reach out and pull themselves to a higher level of existence.

The United States Constitution is said by some to have been modeled in part after the Magna Charta. Perhaps there is truth in that belief. However, the U.S. Constitution was created in a very different way and for very different reasons. The claim can be made that the Constitution is the nobler of the two documents, in that it specifically granted to all men unprecedented dignity and "inalienable rights" previously unheard of (undreamed of by most) anywhere, at any time before in history. Nonetheless, the common thread between these documents is the thread of that most desired of all things, Freedom.

When and where in the history of our planet can anyone find the desire in a people to voluntarily abandon or discard its freedom? Never . . . Nowhere! Freedom, once achieved is never intentionally, thoughtfully cast aside or thrown away. There are, however, many instances where taking freedom for granted, ignoring the responsibilities and duties that always accompany freedom, has resulted in the loss of their freedom to many people all over the globe.

The intent of this essay is not to reopen old wounds from the past. It must be noted, though, that modern and ancient history is replete with examples of peoples who surrendered themselves to a notion that a particular, perceived "Leader" could offer them "security" in some manner, only to find in the end, their freedom but a memory and the promised security lost in the vapors of a failed society or nation.

Furthermore, though most of us use the word freedom in a singular sense, freedom is, in reality a collection of *freedoms* – plural. The response, in this essay, to the question that is the essay's topic is given from the perspective of the author's second generation American citizenship. In America, and elsewhere, freedom consists of a *wide range* of freedoms "of" and freedoms "from". Consider the following partial list of freedoms that are among all of the many individual freedoms we enjoy that, when taken together, form the all encompassing treasure we call FREEDOM. There are: freedom of thought, freedom of speech, freedom of religion, freedom of artistic expression, freedom of academic expression and pursuit, freedom of dissent, freedom of association. Look also at a few of our freedoms from: freedom from oppression, freedom from discrimination, freedom from illegal seizure or search.

We, in America, have so many freedoms, most of which were handed to us with no effort on our part, that we have become soft. We have increasingly abused the freedoms we have, so much so, that we are losing them. That great Tower of Freedom, that enables us to

enjoy good health and a good life, is developing cracks, fractures that, if left unchecked, will ultimately bring down that precious Tower of Freedom, just as surely as our lack of vigilance and neglect of our duty to protect and preserve our freedom resulted in the destruction of the magnificent World Trade Center Towers. Make no mistake. Our freedom can be taken from us if we fail to preserve and protect it...if we fail to pay the price to keep it.

Why then are we reflecting on the question "How Much Freedom Should We Trade For Security?" Can there be any other answer but: "None"? To whom is the question directed? Obviously, the essay topic question has no practical application to a huge percentage of the world's population. Much of Asia and the Middle East consist of nations whose citizens or subjects have very little or no freedom to trade for anything. An individual living in the Peoples Republic of China does not have the option to consider whether or not to trade any freedom for any security.

That person has no freedom to trade, which brings us back to the point raised earlier: without freedom, there is no security; can be no security. If one cannot control one's own life by the exercise of free choices, such as where to live, where to work, whom to associate with and the like, then that individual has no security whatsoever.

Thus, it follows that this essay competition, by virtue of its topical question, is directed to those who reside in what is commonly called "The Free World". Who among us living in the Free World could honestly quarrel with the claim that the threats to our freedom come, mainly, from enemies of freedom who do not live in the Free World. Part of the problem is that of perspective.

Many free people have, for so long, taken freedom for granted, completely neglected their duty to preserve and pay the price of their freedom, that their perspective on the realities of the world and its people has become skewed. They have slipped into a mindset that causes them to misread what is going on in the world and in their lives.

These individuals see the conditions around them from their skewed perspective and come to incorrect conclusions on issues of great importance. Such an individual, for example, regards the terrorist attacks on the World Trade Center and the Pentagon, last September 11, 2001, as a threat to our *security*. Those attacks were attacks on our *freedom*, not our *security*.

The security *deficit* that enabled the terrorists to execute their attacks against America and Freedom was a direct consequence of the fact that we Americans, collectively, failed to protect and preserve our freedom.

We have, as a nation, become soft...even jaded. We do not guard and protect – and pay for our freedoms. Our Judicial system, our schools, even our churches are in a shambles because we, as a people, have become so soft and apathetic. Our lack of resolve, our selfishness, our weak-kneed willingness to "go along to get along"; all of these and more have been silently undermining our freedom.

Now, we come to the point where we must face the realization that we, each and all of us, must create our own security. The "government" cannot. The "government" will not.

Nations of the West and some of the nations of Eastern Europe are on the threshold of seeing their traditions and culture eclipsed within their own borders by third world enemies of free people and institutions. Only a return to the old values of: respect for freedom (and those who paid the supreme price to buy it for us), devotion to duty, and perseverance in the pursuit of noble goals will ensure the continued blessings of freedom we now enjoy

Our security lies not in trading off freedom, but in guarding and protecting every bit of the freedom we have. Giving up freedom will *never* generate security. If we want peace and freedom, we must protect and support freedom. We must fight, to the death if necessary, for justice.

The Second Civil War

Donald J. Cole, May, 2002
Cypress, TX

War is all around us, all over the globe. At no time in our Nation's history have there been more threats to our security and our survival.

America's armed services are engaged all over the world in a noble struggle to preserve our own freedom and to bring the opportunity for lives of freedom to millions of human beings who have never known the blessings of freedom and justice.

Beneath the radar, parallel to all of the armed conflicts and threatened armed hostilities, there is another war, a war of a very different kind, raging within America's own borders.

Americans now, this very moment, are fully engaged in a second Civil War. Unlike the first Civil War in America, this war is not a war between the states. This war, which has deep roots, is a war between the ideologies of the Left and the Right. This is a very insidious and fragmented battle. The fragmentation aspect, however, does nothing to reduce or weaken the intensity or effect of the war on the fabric of the Nation.   Rather, the fragmented character of this war creates a greater

Pervasiveness, of such proportion, that there is virtually no part of our society, no institution, no tradition, that is not immersed in this intense conflict.

At this point, it is incumbent upon me to declare several points to ensure the integrity and clarity of this, and future essays.

As the first order of business, I will state the facts of my personal history and beliefs, the concerns and motivations that have influenced me and convinced me to establish myself as a chronicler of this Second American Civil War.

I declare, without any hesitation, that my essays will be written from my personal perspective, with no effort to be, or appear to be, neutral on the issues. I am a Christian, conservative, patriotic American. I consider America to be the greatest Nation the world has ever seen throughout its entire history. No other Nation, ever, has contributed more to the advancement and welfare of humankind. America has been, since its inception and remains today, the best hope for the world.

I was born an American, because my Irish great-grandparents had the faith and the courage to take their families on an awesome journey to a new world that offered individual dignity, freedom, and justice on a scale the world had never before known. I thank God every day that they brought my grandparents here so that I could one day be born an American. God blessed my family. And God blessed America.

I believe that I have a duty to clearly show my gratitude for the blessings God has showered upon me, upon my family, and upon this great Nation.   I believe it is not enough to be patriotic. More than just being patriotic . . . we must be Patriots.

Anyone who reads my essays and disagrees with my words should feel completely comfortable with his or her right to disagree.

Chinese Saber Rattling Has a Tinny Ring

Donald J. Cole, Cypress, TX

August 28, 2001

Recent media reports have claimed that high ranking Chinese Military leaders have floated the notion that China may launch an attack on an American Aircraft Carrier. I can't find any factual documentation to support the accuracy of the reports. However, if such ideas or threats have, in fact, been expressed by any ChiCom military brass, two words immediately come to my lips: What Crap!

I am frequently amazed these days at the hand wringing, "lions and tigers and bears, Oh My" sissified whimpering of what seems to be a growing number of so-called Americans.

So some twisted Chinese Communist dreamers say they plan to attack an American Carrier, and some wimpy American Utopians are shaking in their booties. Well, remember that the arrogant, Imperialist, IGNORANT Japanese had their own delusional scheme to destroy America in 1941. They paid a supremely high price for their gross stupidity.

Let me tell you something that you should never forget. For all of the lazy, selfish, shiftless, amoral, and cowardly people in this country who would run and hide in the face of such a threat, there are millions of other Americans, some born here, others, like the millions of immigrants, who love this nation and treasure the extraordinary freedoms we enjoy in America - like no other nation in the history of the earth - who would stand and be counted; who would stand and fight; who would be a part of the mighty force that would respond to any such attack and eradicate the Chinese communist scum from the earth, once and for all. (My sincere apologies for the run-on sentence, especially to my fifth grade teacher, Mrs. West)

Many years ago, Harry Truman, who had the good sense to follow the good advice he received and dropped two big bombs on Japan that saved hundreds of thousands, perhaps millions of lives - Japanese lives, as well as Americans and others of our Allies. Those two big bombs ended the horror and atrocities of the war in the Pacific. Those two big bombs put a huge exclamation point to the message the Japanese finally absorbed: "Stupid Bastards; you underestimated the people of the United States of America".

Had Harry Truman not allowed himself to get into an ego "pissing contest" with General Mac Arthur in Korea, and let him bomb the hell out of the Chinese then, there would have never been a Viet Nam war and Zemin and his flunkies would not be doing this ridiculous posturing now. **China**: BEWARE the sleeping tiger that ate the Japanese dragon!

Charity Begins At Home . . . Doesn't It?

Donald J. Cole, Page 1 of 5

©June 1998, Cypress, TX

I'll strap on a tin beak and peck s- -t with the chickens if it will earn me a paycheck". I heard that crude statement many times in my younger days. I'm sure I said it myself, more than once. As crude, even vulgar, as the statement may be, the words reveal much about the speaker. The words say that the speaker is a person who will do whatever it takes to earn an honest paycheck.

I haven't heard that statement in years. Nor have I seen much evidence of folks with the determination of the speakers of bygone days, who uttered the words. People then made the statement to say they would take any work, however much below their station; no matter how demeaning it appeared, in order to earn their way, feed and clothe their families, and keep a roof over their heads.

What I observe these days, and especially around major holidays, like Thanksgiving and Christmas, are people who want someone else to rescue them from their self perceived "plight". A victim mentality prevails these days among an alarmingly growing number of Americans. So many people claim to be victims of this, that, or the other. Some seem to revel in their self-declared victim status. Many of these poor, helpless unfortunates, as they are described to us by the news media, church hierarchies, and community service organizations, are not as helpless as it may appear.

They are more helpless, it seems, at sniffing out potential places of employment than they are at locating the burgeoning number of venues handing out free food, clothes and other items. They seem unable to grasp the essence of the dignity and satisfaction that comes from doing a hard day's work, earning a paycheck and paying their own way.

No doubt some, having gone this far into what I am writing, will have decided that I am a heartless, insensitive, uncaring man, with no charity in his heart. Not so. I care very much about the plight of the truly poor, aged and infirm. I gladly give of my time, talent and treasure. Unfortunately though, what I see happening in cities all over the nation is a movement

that passes off, as poor and unfortunate, tens of thousands of able-bodied people who are totally capable of securing work and earning a paycheck; people who choose to seek charity *instead* of work.

This movement, as I see it, is orchestrated and choreographed by a relatively small number of so-called leaders. Some of these so-called leaders are sincere in their belief they are working to help the poor and downtrodden in our midst. Others of these so-called leaders, though, do not pursue a noble cause. Power is the goal they seek; ever increasing power. And they use every bit of power they gain to promote their own selfish goals, to gain more and more power and influence.

Hordes of decent, charitable people are urged into the movement by these so-called leaders; mobilized to collect food, clothing and other goods to be distributed among the alleged, ever-growing numbers of poor unfortunates. These same volunteers are, daily, manning the soup kitchens, food and clothing distribution centers, and other handout venues frequented by the people the so-called leaders declare to be poor unfortunates. Charity is not what this process is. Rather, this process, already out of control, is a deadly cancer in our country.

Of the tens, perhaps hundreds, of thousands of people across America who receive these handouts, a substantial number are people who should be working and earning paychecks, supporting their families.

In earlier times, a husband/father who could not earn enough money from his job to provide for all the needs of his family, went out and found a second job; in some cases, even a third job. His wife, the mother of their children stayed at home and created a warm, loving environment for the family. She prepared their meals, kept the home clean and inviting, washed and ironed clothes, nursed her husband or children when they were sick. She made their home, however modest, into their family refuge, filled with love, devotion and honor.

Both the husband/father and the wife/mother worked hard to build and sustain the family. If it required long working hours and personal sacrifices to provide for the family's needs, the hours were worked and the sacrifices made for the welfare of the family. Personal desires and wishes were fulfilled only after the needs of the family were met. Phrases like "quality time" did not exist. All hours spent by the members of the family with each other were quality time, as were the working hours spent by husband/fathers and wife/mothers at their respective tasks for the welfare of the family.

That does not happen today in many, if not most, American households. It is a national tragedy of enormous proportions that there are so many single parent households. Divorce and promiscuity are the major reasons for the single parent phenomenon. Selfishness, a pervasive sense of entitlement to anything one wants, is at the root of both the promiscuity and the divorce problem.

THE COLLECTED LETTERS

AN OPEN LETTER TO THE U. S. CONFERENCE OF CATHOLIC BISHOPS

His Eminence
Francis Cardinal George

Archbishop of Chicago

President, United States
Conference of Catholic
Bishops

3211 Fourth Street NE

Washington, DC 20017-1194

June 15, 2010

PREFACE

I have read many times in recent years a phrase that appears to be emerging as a standard in some quarters, when reporting on letters of concerns or complaint sent to prominent individuals or organizations by citizens or groups. The phrase is: " . . . in a rambling letter sent to . . .". I once received a reply letter from a Bishop who took offense to my "broadside" (his word). In my own reply to him, I explained that I did not issue a broadside, but had carefully chosen my words to communicate my well intended critical comments regarding certain subjects associated with developments in our Holy Mother Church, that I found very troubling.

The subjects I wish to address here, in this letter, are very important, timely and troubling to me . . . and, I am certain, to at least thousands (perhaps millions) of other Catholics. However, this letter is my own. I represent no group or movement. Nor will the words I write here be "talking points" or any such prepared remarks fed to me by anyone else.

I am a lifelong Catholic. I love God. I love my family. I love my Church. I love my Country. I make my best effort to give this letter structure and organized form in presenting my points, so as to discourage anyone from characterizing it as "a rambling letter to the USCCB" (The Bishops).

By way of Outline, this letter will be constructed as follows:

- Biographical/Historical notes on the writer
- The Problems - Subject Issues and concerns
- The Particulars
- A call for Leadership

BIOGRAPHICAL/HISTORICAL NOTES ON THE WRITER

Allow me to introduce myself and set the tone for the remarks I will offer in this letter. My name is Donald J. Cole. I am a Catholic. I was a Catholic for many years before many of you who are members of the USCCB were born. I was baptized shortly after my birth in April 1935 in the Brooklyn, NY Diocese and Confirmed as a Soldier of Christ at the age of eleven. Today, at age seventy-five, I remain steadfast in my faith as the Soldier of Christ I became as a young boy shortly after the conclusion of World War II. For over fifty-four years I have shared my life with Patsy Jean (Carter) Cole, the exceptional woman who became my wife, at Resurrection Parish in Brooklyn on January 7, 1956. Patsy was not a Catholic on that day, thus we were not permitted to have a Mass or be married on the Altar. We came to the Altar rail on that day with total and absolute love for each other and complete commitment to the vows we made to God and to each other. We fulfilled the biblical description of marriage and, indeed, we two, became as one. We have three children and seven grandchildren. Patsy became a convert to the Catholic Church in 1970 and was Confirmed at St. Thomas More parish in the Galveston-Houston Diocese.

For more than forty years, I have served as a Minister of the Word, one of the members of the first class of Lectors trained at St. Mary's Seminary in Houston. Patsy and I are both Extraordinary Ministers of the Holy Eucharist. I am a Fourth Degree Member of The Knights of Columbus; a proud and Patriotic American Catholic.

THE PROBLEMS - SUBJECT ISSUES AND CONCERNS

On this day in June, 2010, the entire world faces an extraordinary array of problems. Armies of writers could spend every waking hour creating volumes of material identifying and defining the almost endless list of threats and dangers facing humankind. That is not the intent or purpose of this letter. I wish to present a list of seven specific problems, in all of which, I believe the USCCB is involved. In this section, I will present my list as concisely as I am able to. I have done my best to distill the extensive number of issues and concerns that I view as troubling and a threat to our Church and our Country. I have stated my position as a Patriotic American Catholic. You should rightly expect my words to resonate from that context.

The following list is not ranked in a perceived order of importance or urgency. I hold the position that each of the items on the list is as urgent and dangerous as each of the other items.

- THE RIGHT TO LIFE
- PRAYER
- RELIGIOUS FREEDOM
- CATHOLIC RELIGIOUS OBLIGATIONS OF GOVERNMENT/ELECTED REPRESENTATIVES/APPOINTEES/BUREAUCRACY
- CATHOLIC RELIGIOUS OBLIGATIONS OF CITIZENS/RESIDENTS
- CATHOLIC OBLIGATIONS REGARDING THE LAWS OF THE LAND
- RESTORING AND PRESERVING CATHOLIC TRADITION AND COURAGE IN THE CHURCH

THE PARTICULARS

In this section, I will present details of what I believe to be troubling and/or threatening about the subject item and my own humble – but critical comments on the USCCB's and/or the Laity's failings in the day to day actions or lack of actions related to the subject. I wish to strongly emphasize here that I hold no delusions of grandeur. I am but a single, simple man with no authority or power, beyond that of any other man or woman, to change the Church, the Country, or anyone in either of those institutions. Yet, I believe and accept

234

that I have a duty to God, the Church, the Country, and my fellow man to have the courage to stand and proclaim any and all conditions that exist as threats or dangers to these institutions I hold close to my heart. I have, on occasion, been ridiculed for standing up to defend the values that I believe in, and which I believe I am obliged to defend. I will always risk ridicule to stand for what I believe is right. That said, I now offer the particulars of the Problems I have identified above.

THE RIGHT TO LIFE

For thirty-seven years, since the Supreme Court's Roe vs. Wade Decision, an American Holocaust has raged on. More than fifty million babies have been exterminated – either in the mother's womb or at a point where the child was actually partially born. Yes, you read it correctly . . . I said, "Child". Abortion supporters claim that a baby in the womb is not a baby at all, but merely a "fetus" , the property of the mother, who has every right to do with "it" as she wishes. As a Catholic Christian, I reject and condemn that position. I have several fundamental differences with such a notion. First and foremost, I take exception with the idea that the baby ("fetus") belongs to the mother – especially during the gestation period when he or she is growing and receiving nutrition from conception to birth by the natural process of God's own creation, independent of anything the so-called mother does except an act intended to hurt or destroy the child. The baby is God's property until through the birthing process, the child is given to the woman by God and the woman's status changes from expectant mother to mother. In fact, the child – from conception, throughout life and until death – is NEVER the property of the "mother", but rather, a gift to the woman from God.

The USCCB frequently proclaim that they support the right to life. Statements condemning abortion are released repeatedly by USCCB. Those proclamations and statements have not brought an end to the carnage and it is no surprise that the slaughter of the innocent babies continues. Words, homilies and pleadings will not bring an end to the disgraceful massacre. Action is what is needed. Such action, rightly, should originate with the Bishops – the Leaders, the Princes of the Church. Courage is what is needed from the Bishops. Where is the courage of our Bishops? What ACTION has the USCCB taken to end the sin of abortion?

Cardinal George's letter to Barak Obama after he was elected, and before he was inaugurated, offered the prayers of the Catholic Bishops of the United States and urged Obama to embrace policies respecting life in his administration. Obama's brazen, arrogant response was quick. In his first week in office it was announced that his administration would provide American tax dollars to fund abortion in foreign lands. In early March, 2009 he provided an exclamation point to his response to Cardinal George's letter, proclaiming that he will lift the ban on embryonic stem cell research.

If the Cardinal's letter was intended to elicit a response that would clearly show the world where Obama stands on respect for life, it succeeded on that point. But the net effect was that the letter was a wasted effort. Had the Cardinal, instead, cautioned Obama to tread carefully on respect for life issues or risk invoking the wrathful backlash of Christian America, we might have seen a better result.

The reality of the dilemma, however, appears to reside in the perception by many that the Bishops do not deliver strong leadership, and that many Catholics are ambivalent on life issues. Obama's comment: "Words . . . just words" would likely define his opinion of the Bishops' leadership. The unacceptable number of counterfeit Catholic elected officials in powerful government positions, unchallenged officially, for all practical purposes would appear to support such a hypothesis.

It is well past the time for the Bishops to take stern and decisive action to clearly back up their Pro-life claims and demonstrate to the Catholic laity and all Americans the leadership that is their duty.

It is common knowledge that in poll after poll, results reveal that large percentages of Catholics are at odds with the Church's teaching on the right to life. I attribute that sad condition to the Bishops' failure to have the courage to be soldiers of Christ and defend the Church from the enemies of God who are trying desperately to destroy it. If Catholics are to unite in defense of the right to life, they must have courageous and strong leadership . . . bold leadership! That is the Bishops' duty.

PRAYER

Prayer, most particularly, Christian prayer is under intense attack in America from many quarters, both inside and outside our borders. So-called Atheists and others, including radical Islamists will never cease in the efforts to destroy all vestiges of Christian religion and culture. Jesus Christ, our Lord and Savior has been driven out of the schools – where our children's minds and values are formed . . . and from all public places.

Recently, a twisted Federal Judge ruled that the National Day of Prayer is unconstitutional - did you read that? UNCONSTITUTIONAL! How dare this woman commit such a disgraceful act to mock the faith and the wisdom of those who founded this Nation and WROTE the Constitution? Yes, there is an appeal process ongoing. But where is the outcry? Where are the prominent and powerful exclamations of outrage? Where are the calls to remove this person from the Federal Bench?

Another recent event saw the Reverend Franklin Graham disinvited by the Army to offer a prayer during the National Day Of Prayer ceremony at the Pentagon. Why? Because some Christianity hater claimed the Reverend Graham insulted muslims with comments he made in the past about the historical acts and teachings of muslims. The charges are baseless and offensive to Christians everywhere. Yet, the action stood – a disgrace to the United States Army and to the United States. Where is the Action from the Bishops? Why have the Bishops not risen to their feet and demanded apology for these acts. If we tolerate such offensive and insulting actions, what are we? What are the Bishops?

Some years ago, when there was a rash of attacks on prayer in America, I started to work on establishing a grass roots organization: "We Will Pray". The mission of the organization was to be very simple: to gather in small groups or as individuals, to go to public places and meetings, stand and pray; or to encourage our children to stand in class in the morning and pray aloud. If the child should be silenced or sent home, the parents would accompany the child the next day and stand with him or her and pray. Yes, I am aware that is civil disobedience. I was unable to complete the organization at the time.

I recently sent an email to 101 individuals in my address book, inviting those who were interested in establishing the "We Will Pray" organization to send a three word response: "Count me in".

Two of the emails I sent were undeliverable. Of the 99 that were received, I received three of the three word responses and no others.

I sent a follow up message stating that I considered "no response" to be a response – a rather emphatic response, actually. If the Bishops will not rise and demand our right to prayer, why would our laity have the courage to do so?

RELIGIOUS FREEDOM

Separation of Church and State   There are no such words in the United States Constitution.
Article III of The Articles of Confederation states:

"The said states hereby severally enter into a firm league of friendship with each other, for their common defence, the security of their Liberties, and their mutual and general welfare, binding themselves to assist each other, against all force offered to, or attacks made upon them, or any of them, on account of religion, sovereignty, trade, or any other pretence whatever."

The first Amendment states:

"Congress shall make no law respecting establishment of religion, or prohibiting the free exercise thereof; or abridging the freedom of speech, or of the press; or the right of the people peaceably to assemble, and to petition the government for a redress of grievances."

Can any thinking individual with a functioning brain fail to see and understand that our freedom of religion is under severe attack by an array of enemies – and especially enemies within our own country – and most especially from renegade elements of our own government?

The founding documents of our country, the words and papers of our founders and early leaders are filled with eloquent references and acknowledgements of the fact that our nation is a Christian Nation whose laws and institutions were created under the guidance and teachings of Jesus Christ. That said, we are nonetheless a nation dedicated to religious tolerance, as richly evidenced by the huge number and variety of places of worship in our beloved America – a Nation with neither peer nor equal, with respect to religious freedom.

Yet, we find our Christian institutions and traditions, those same institutions and traditions upon which our country was built, continually under ever growing attack. We must put an end to the disrespect and the persecution without delay. Without a strong defense and practice of our Christian beliefs in all phases of American everyday life, our Christian religion will wither and die.

Again, I call upon the Bishops to set the example and Lead.

CATHOLIC RELIGIOUS OBLIGATIONS OF GOVERNMENT ELECTED REPRESENTATIVES/APPOINTEES/ BUREAUCRACY

Nearly six years ago, on October 25, 2004, just days before the National General Elections in the United States, I wrote a letter to Archbishop Joseph Fiorenza, who was then Bishop of the Galveston-Houston Diocese and I believe, if my memory serves me correctly, also President of the USCCB. My letter was precipitated by an event at my Parish Church on Sunday, September 12, when the so-called "Social Justice" ministry of St. Anne's Parish, Tomball, Texas, conducted a voter register drive after the Masses. I was offended by a T-shirt worn by one of the Social Justice ministry members that was emblazoned with the statement "Fair U.S. Elections . . . brought to you by the International monitors of Pax Christi International".

I offer you the following quote from my letter to Bishop Fiorenza:

(Quote) . . . I will state, without fear of any credible contradiction, that America stands alone in the world of nations as the beacon of freedom for all other nations to follow, where free and fair elections are the only kind of elections we conduct. The Marxist, America hating, baseless blather of the left to the contrary, we neither need nor welcome any international monitors from the left wing Pax Christi or any other America hating organization to ensure free and fair elections.

As a lifelong, practicing Catholic soldier of Christ, I am deeply offended that Pax Christi, the so-called "Catholic" organization dares to demean the memory and the sacrifice of the millions of Americans who sacrificed their very lives to protect and preserve America's free and fair elections. I would be doubly offended to learn that the USCCB had a hand in such behavior. Please tell me it is not true.

If, in fact, it is true, Bishop, I would have to say that the Bishops and the USCCB would be better advised to use their leadership position to counsel Catholics not to scandalize themselves or the Church by voting for "Counterfeit Catholic" politicians who run for high office, than to insinuate that we don't have fair elections.

By "Counterfeit Catholics" I refer, of course, to those politicians who, as if their earlier treasonous activities against our nation were not harmful enough, also scandalize Catholics and our Church. Such arrogant, morally bankrupt politicians, while proclaiming themselves to the world to be Catholics, brazenly stand in defiance of Catholic doctrine and teaching, and even Papal authority.

These men and women flagrantly proclaim, support, endorse and advocate such issues as the culture of

243

death of abortion, euthanasia, and other perversions, such as homosexual "marriage".

You know who these defenders of the culture of death, the promoters of perversion are. They are people like John Kerry, Nancy Pelosi, Tom Daschel, Teddy Kennedy, and numerous others of their ilk. I believe twenty-four of them recently signed a letter to the American Bishops, boldly warning the Bishops, in so many words, to "butt out". How utterly sad, to see.

The Bishops, who should be steadfast defenders of the Church, and leaders of the Faithful, have allowed (with a few courageous exceptions) such sinful behavior to go – not just unpunished – but unchallenged. How do faithful Catholics explain to our non-Catholic friends and neighbors (and our children as well) the failure of the Bishops to defend and lead our Holy Mother Church.

I have lived too long to expect much good to come from politicians of any stripe. But I still expect to see more than I do from our Bishops.

The scandals of recent years that have bedeviled our Church did not happen overnight, or in a vacuum. Bishop, you know that, I know that, and every thinking Catholic knows that. I see clear parallels between the moral decay reflected in the Church's scandals and the cancerous decline of morality in large parts of our national population. Those parallels lead back to the same approximate starting point in time – the mid-sixties when, in the wake of Vatican II, the wave of left wing permissiveness and perversion gave rise to the variety of destructive beliefs and behaviors that have taken such a huge toll upon the moral character of our people, both in and outside of the Church.

Though I am not one to submit to despair, I do not expect this little letter to have any substantial impact on you or the USCCB. In all candor, I honestly feel that my words here will fall upon deaf ears and that you will essentially turn a blind eye to this letter. But it was important to me and absolutely necessary that I write it. . . . (End Quote)

In his reply to my letter, Bishop Fiorenza characterized my October 25, 2004 letter as a "broadside" at Bishops in general. I offer you the following quote from my November 7, 2004 response to Bishop Fiorenza:

(Quote) . . . I'm sorry that what you characterized as my "broadside" at Bishops in general offended you. I did not write to offend. And I do not wish to come across now as antagonistic. However, I speak and write as clearly as I can to express my convictions, values, and beliefs. I do not spend time searching for touchy-feely, or so-called politically- correct terminology. I have numerous deeply held concerns about the Church I hold so dear to my heart. I believe God calls all of us to stand up and speak out for our beliefs, and for His Church. I try my best to do that.

In the wake of the election, and in the context of your document, "Together In His Name", I have more that I would like to write. However, beyond one brief comment on your document I will not use this letter to present my case, as it were. What I will state here is that you wrote in paragraph three of Together In His Name: "As Bishops, we seek to form the consciences of our people". Mr. Kerry's victory, in all of the states he managed to win, came from approximately twenty percent of the total number of counties in each of those states, states like Massachusetts, New York, and Pennsylvania (the state with the largest number of Catholic voters). Interestingly, as well, those counties Kerry won also happen to have the highest number of Catholics in them. I would submit to you, with all due respect, that it certainly appears that the Bishops did not succeed in forming the consciences of those particular Catholics, and I believe I know several reasons why. I am working on an essay. I will send you a copy when it is completed, in case you would be interested in reading it. . . .(End Quote).

Now . . . today, in June, 2010, the same counterfeit Catholics continue to occupy elected positions in our government, appointed positions in the administration and countless numbers of bureaucracy positions. Of course we now have the added dimension of the frightening number of Marxist, Socialist, Communist, Atheist and Radical Islamists who occupy positions alongside many of the counterfeit Catholics. I would speculate that some. Perhaps many, of the counterfeit Catholics may be Communists, Marxists and Socialists as well.

Where, Sirs, is the leadership from the USCCB? Am I, and what I believe to be millions of other American Catholics unreasonable in our expectations that our Bishops should have – must have – the courage to stand up against the extraordinary behaviors of prominent Catholics in the government who figuratively spit in the face of the Bishops and defile Catholic teaching in the halls of government for all the world to see? WHERE IS THE LEADERSHIP? WHERE IS YOUR COMMITMENT TO YOUR DUTY TO DEFEND THE CHURCH?

All Catholic elected government representatives . . . as well as Administration appointees and bureaucrats should be put on notice that, their active - or passive – participation in promoting, endorsing, supporting, or conducting Abortion activity violates Catholic teaching and places them at risk of excommunication from the Church. Those who choose to continue such activity should be promptly -   and prominently - excommunicated.

Jesus said to the Apostles: "Whose sins you shall forgive, they are forgiven. Whose sins you shall retain, they are retained." I have proclaimed the words of Holy Scripture, as a Lector, for more than forty years and take my responsibility very seriously. I study the words I will read and do research to reveal what the words mean to me, in order to present them as faithfully as I can, so that the congregation might find and feel what those words mean to each of them.   My own understanding of the meaning of Jesus' words, quoted above is simply that there are sins that can only be forgiven by God in His infinite wisdom, and not by His Priests. I believe the sins of the Counterfeit Catholics in our government, sins that so gravely injure the Church and the Faithful are such sins, and must be punished.

CATHOLIC RELIGIOUS OBLIGATIONS OF CITIZENS/RESIDENTS

It is well established that growing numbers of Catholics in America and throughout most of the world do not fulfill their religious obligations as they should. Attendance at Mass is disturbingly low. Knowledge of our Faith and the Teachings of the Church is very poor. Reception of the Sacraments to many Catholics is relatively meaningless. Catholics and many other Christians seem to be inured to the moral and cultural evils of the world and unconcerned about their duty to God. The divorce rates of Catholics are astonishing.

Living together outside of wedlock is considered to be normal and practical to many young – and older – Catholics. In many respects, our Holy Mother Church is falling   apart.

The Priestly scandals have so scarred the Church in the eyes of the world . . . and more importantly, in the eyes of Catholics, that the Holy Father publicly asks the world for forgiveness and pledges that these horrible transgressions will never be repeated.

I propose to you that the sad state of the Catholic Church and of the so-called Faithful has grown out of the failure of our Church Leadership to actually Lead, and Lead By Example. The leadership has allowed the Church to become so secularized and allowed so many of the sacred traditions to be thrown out of the Church, that the Church, when compared to earlier times, such as the first half of the twentieth century, is almost unrecognizable.

Catholics fail in their religious obligations. To restore the Church, Catholics must return to the practice of the Faith. Many Catholics blame their failure to meet their obligations on the Church and its Leaders. Is there anyone who cannot imagine why they take that position? But that position is false! That position doesn't hold water. That position is a consequence of their own personal failure to have the courage to live the Faith and do their duty to God and their families and neighbors, out of their own love for their savior, Jesus Christ, who died that all of us may live. We all have a duty to live our faith with or without the assistance of the Leaders of the Church.

The truth, however, reveals that the failure of the Faithful has its roots in the failure of the Bishops. How many Bishops have the remotest understanding of what the average hard working Catholic family must deal with in today's world?

I am not referring to Catholics in abject poverty. The number of Bishops throughout the world who could honestly claim to have a true understanding of that life condition would be a very small number.

The point I wish to make here is not that Bishops should have to live in poverty, or anything close to it. But too many of the Bishops live a life of privilege surrounded by luxury. We need to see the Bishops develop a toughness they seem not to have and the courage to stand up without hesitation and actually fight the enemies of the Church.

If the Bishops stood side by side and publicly called for Catholics to flood the government with phone calls, letters, faxes, emails and live demonstrations demanding an end to the culture of death, the trashing of religious expression and all such ills, that demonstration of strength and courage would transfer to the Faithful very quickly.

I have long believed that there should be a Bishops' Boot Camp, where new Bishops would be trained – up close and personal – to learn and understand the realities of everyday life for the Faithful and the struggles and challenges thrust upon them by the secular world in which we live. I believe the Bishops, the Faithful and the Church would be the better for it.

I truly believe that people, all people, WANT to be GOOD people. But most people need an example of how to achieve that condition.

CATHOLIC OBLIGATIONS REGARDING THE LAWS OF THE LAND

There is a virtual tsunami of illegal immigrant invaders flowing into the United States and wreaking havoc with much of our infrastructure, especially with our medical facilities, schools and public welfare resources. I will not use this space to construct a list of tables and graphs to illustrate the massive amounts of money and resources that are being literally stolen from the American people daily, and mostly in the states along our southern border.

America is a great and generous nation that has always welcomed the immigrant. There was a time when the immigrants fortunate enough to reach our shores had a common goal they wanted to achieve - to become Americans. The immigrants came to America to have the opportunity to make a better life for themselves and their families. I, myself, am but a second generation American. All four of my grandparents were immigrants – legal immigrants. Most immigrants to America still come here to escape intolerable conditions in their native country and find a better life.

But there are differences today, as well, from those immigrants of earlier times; serious differences that threaten our way of life and our security. Many of today's immigrants, too many of them, do not come here with the common goal of becoming an American. They come here, instead, to establish satellites of their native countries within our American borders.

This is very wrong and a threat to our Culture. I will not go into the specifics here of that part of the problem. Instead, I will focus on the illegal invaders crossing our borders . . . and what I consider to be the disgraceful behavior in some quarters of our Catholic Church and of some of our Bishops.

America is a nation of laws. The Bible teaches us that we are to give unto Caesar what is Caesar's. It is not the province of the Church to dictate to the United States or any subdivision of the United States how to enact or enforce its laws. The laws of our country are just. They are not perfect, just as nothing else is perfect. There are many in our Nation and in our Church, working constantly to destroy our Constitutional system of Fair and Just Laws. They are enemies of God, the Church and our nation.

Moreover, we have a growing situation in America today that sees the elements of Church acting in complicity with criminal, illegal alien invaders and organizations that sponsor them. That is a sin. Aiding and abetting criminal activity is a SIN. And sinful activity begets sinful activity. Even worse, hearing a Cardinal of the Catholic Church prominently and publicly trashing the people of the State of Arizona - good hard-working, honest Americans (many of whom are Catholic) – calling them Nazis and Communists because they wish to see the Fair and Just Laws of the United States enforced, is an unredeemable disgrace.

I will not mince words here . . . Cardinal Mahony's reprehensible comments demeaning my fellow Americans in Arizona reveal his complete failure. He should be forced into retirement immediately. Or will we see the day when the Holy Father feels the need to publicly ask forgiveness for such behavior by the Leadership (?) of the Catholic Church.

Too many of the so-called leaders in our Church – *and other Churches as well*, with whom some of our Leaders have aligned themselves, are applying a twisted logic the notion that all humans have a "Right to migrate". That is true only with respect to "Legal Migration". No one has the *right* to migrate illegally.

The Bishops need to wake up and live in the real world. Those in the Church who sponsor, encourage, support, provide money and sanctuary, and participate in the criminal illegal alien invasion of our country will come face to face on Judgment Day with the fact that they must answer for the many people they effectively drove away from the Church – people who could not in good conscience reconcile with the Church's complicity in criminal acts. This is a serious transgression of God's law.

RESTORING AND PRESERVING CATHOLIC TRADITION AND COURAGE IN THE CHURCH

With a number of outstanding exceptions, as a group, the U. S. Conference Of Catholic Bishops have shown a great lack of the courage to defend the Church from our enemies; enemies within and outside the Church. The result has been that a great number of our faithful traditions and practices have been thrown out of the Church, to the dismay and disgust of millions of Catholics.

It is time to stop the bleeding. I believe there are millions of Catholics who are waiting for the call from the Bishops to rid the Church of the usurpers who have damaged and dismantled so much of our beloved Church and will not stop until they are exposed and expelled or they succeed in their mission.

Courage is contagious.

PLEASE. Stand up, Bishops, and display the courage we need to restore and preserve the Church. If there is a Bishop who feels incapable of mustering such courage, he should have the integrity to resign his position to a man that does.

With my sincere prayers that God may bless you and guide you in your vocation, I am,
Respectfully,
Donald J. Cole, Cypress, TX

Letter to Francis Cardinal George, OMI

President, United States Conference of Catholic Bishops

Donald J. Cole,   March 9, 2009

Cypress, TX

His Eminence Francis Cardinal George, OMI

Archbishop of Chicago

President, United States Conference of Catholic Bishops

3211 Fourth Street NE

Washington, DC 20017-1194

Your Eminence,

Allow me to say as preface to my following remarks, that I write this letter to you as a lifelong practicing Catholic who holds you, in your office of Priest, Archbishop, and Cardinal, in complete respect. However, in all candor, I must say that my respect for you does not extend to your office of President of the

USCCB. If you perceive any of my comments here to be written out of dis-respect, I assure you, Your Eminence, that such a perception would be, solely, the result of a misinterpretation of my words. If it seems I am belaboring this point, it is because a letter of mine to one of your predecessors was viewed thusly and communicated to me in a biting response.

May I also say here that I recognize the difficult position you occupy as President of USCCB. Much is expected and demanded of the man who fills the position. I believe only one who is up to the significant challenges of the position should either seek or accept the position, and that our Lord will look not for him to be a great man, but to do great deeds.

I read the letter you wrote, dated January 16, 2009, to Barack Obama, after his election and before his inauguration. In your letter, you assured Obama of the prayers of The Catholic Bishops of the United States.

You went on to urge Obama to embrace policies respecting life in his administration. It did not take long for you to receive the first part of Obama's response to your letter, when it was announced during his first week in office that his administration would provide American tax dollars to fund abortion in foreign lands. More recently, this week, Obama has proclaimed that he will lift the ban on embryonic stem cell research.

Do you now, Cardinal George, believe you have received Obama's response to your January 16, 2009 letter? Can Obama make any plainer his repudiation of the requests you made of him, and the goodwill you expressed in your letter? Barack Hussein Obama is an enemy of the Catholic Church and of decent, faithful Christians and others of various faiths. In short, Obama does not respect LIFE.   Obama is a disciple of the culture of death. Surely, you must now understand that fact.

I stated above that my respect for you did not extend to your position as President of the USCCB. Please allow me to explain why. As the leader of our Nation's Catholic Bishops, I believe you bear the responsibility of doing everything possible to advance and protect the teachings of Holy Mother Church in all aspects of everyday life in America, a heavy burden to be sure. However, I believe you have, as have some of your predecessors, failed to deal with the counterfeit Catholic individuals who hold high office in our United States government. These individuals – and they are not just a few minor players – present themselves to the world as Catholics, but brazenly flaunt the teachings of the Church and of Papal authority. These individuals, you know who they are, not only accept the practice of abortion and other culture of death practices, but go well beyond that to endorse and promote such practices as partial birth abortion, which is nothing less than Infanticide! These despicable frauds, true enemies of our faith, bring grave disgrace to the Catholic Church throughout the world.

Have you given any thought, Cardinal George, to the devastating effect of your failure to demand appropriate disciplinary measures against these fraudulent Catholic impostors in our government, on everyday Catholics throughout our Country? I can tell you that Catholics all over America are demoralized by the lack of any action by the Leadership (USCCB) to hold these fraudulent Catholic politicians and other government officials accountable for their actions. Like many Catholics I know, Cardinal George, I am

258

disappointed in the lack of real leadership by the USCCB. I feel abandoned by your failure to stand up and defend the Church against these enemies who mock Catholic teaching and values and bring disgrace upon us.

When will we see the Bishops take positive action to defend the Church against our many enemies – enemies within and outside the Church who would destroy us?

As an eleven-year-old boy in Brooklyn, when Bishop Molloy gently slapped my face (as was then the custom) upon my receipt of the Sacrament of Confirmation, to remind me that I had then become a soldier of Christ, and must be ready to suffer in service to Him, I took the message to heart. I consider myself today, sixty-three years later, that same soldier of Christ I was commissioned to be on that long ago day. Now I ask: what of you, Cardinal? Are you a soldier of Christ? I am aware from first hand personal experiences that many Priests and Bishops in the Post Vatican II Church reject the notion of one being a soldier of Christ. Some of those individuals also have long since discarded the sacrificial aspect of Holy Mass and replaced it with the more palatable (to them and their followers) Celebration of the Eucharist. There are so many little subtleties in our Church today that mask or camouflage what I propose to you is a systematic dismantling and weakening of the infrastructure of the Church and its historical practices, traditions and beliefs. Do you feel an obligation to defend the Church against her brazen enemies, who would destroy the Church and its teachings?

Why do the Bishops persist in submitting the Church to outrageous insult and offense? When may we expect to see the USCCB (and its leader) stand up in prominent defense of the Church against the ever increasing attacks from Her enemies, within and without. Why have the Bishops not issued official notices of intent to excommunicate all of the prominent so-called Catholic Politicians who support, endorse and even promote anti-life legislation - and then take the required steps to carry out the action?

Why, instead of writing letters to the likes of Barack Hussein Obama asking for action that you should well know he has no intention of taking, do you not stand up as a Leader and, instead, demand that he honor and respect life, reverse all anti-life policies and make respect for life a cornerstone of his administration's policies – or face the wrath of the millions of American Catholics.

Why not, instead, warn Mr. Obama that he risks the consequence of millions of Catholics descending, en masse, upon Washington demanding that he alter his administration and turn away from the culture of death in favor of respect for life, or face a concerted effort to have him removed from office? What do you suppose might happen if you, as president of the USCCB, called for all Catholics to join together and descend upon the Capitol and demand a reversal of the administration's policies on life issues? Do you think a million, or five million, or ten million Catholics descending upon the Capitol would make an impact? And do you think others of many different faiths would join with us in that cause?

Are you bold enough . . .and brave enough, Your Eminence, to take such courageous actions to stem the tide of our despicable American Holocaust – fifty million and counting?   I will pray for you every day.

Sincerely yours in Christ,

Response to Willie and Archie...Dubai Ports Deal

Donald J. Cole,   February 22, 2006
Cypress, TX

[*Author's Note: This essay was originally written as a post on the USS Yorktown web site; part of the back and forth banter between two former Yorktown (WWII crewmen) and me (Korean War crewman). Our frequent posts often conflicted. Willie and Archie revered Harry Truman. I did not. That fact ensured that most of our posts to, or in reply to, one another were usually pretty testy. Willie and Archie's dander was especially raised when I reminded them that their revered "War Time President had declared the Korean War, which cost the lives of about 50,000 of America's courageous troops, - A "POLICE ACTION". SURE, POLICE CHIEF HARRY!*]

My response to you, Willie and Archie – and anyone else who does not think this Ports deal stinks:

But first, I have to call you again, Archie, for your usual "cheap shot artist" posts. It appears you don't have the starch to post anything on this board without making reference to "one . . . who labeled a war time President a traitor". Anyone who follows the blather on this board (and I'll include mine, too, because I always seem to take the bait when you post your tripe) will know that you are referring only to me with that tired old trash. They would also know that I have never labeled any President as a traitor – not your saint Harry, or any of the other Democrat feather merchants who have occupied the office.

Now, as to this Port deal. I don't know any more than you do who all of the administration insiders are, who orchestrated this sorry deal. But it is garbage for more reasons than that the UAE cannot rightly be considered to be friends of America.

Friends of America don't recognize the Taliban as the legitimate government of Afghanistan, for example. The UAE is just as duplicitous as all the rest of the Arab countries. And they will try to put up a good front to us in order to grab this peachy deal. Our President is not being well served by the hacks that are promoting this deal, and he should do the wise thing and kill the deal before it becomes an albatross issue.

That ANY *foreign company* (Much less a *foreign government owned company)* should have a contract to control the operations of *ANY* American port is disgusting, to say the least. (And that includes the Brit company, P&O I think it is, that has had the contract for some years) American ports should be run by American companies - and I mean AMERICAN companies – not any of these Multinational Masqueraders that we are overrun with these days.

I don't know what you two birds would like to see for your children's and grand-children's futures, if you have children and grand-children, but I would like mine to have a future to look forward to in an AMERICAN America.

We are at a crossroads in our country today – worse than the one our ancestors faced at the time of the war-between- the- states. The stakes are greater today, and the dangers much graver. Like so many great civilizations before us, e.g. the Greeks, the Romans; we appear to be on a suicidal course to self-destruction.

If that's what you two want for America, you're entitled. But it's not what I want, and enough people speaking against this stinking Port deal might convince the President that he needs to listen to the people and not a handful of "one-worlder" political con artists.

Be well, you old goats.[1]

1   A TERM OF ENDEARMENT FOR THESE TWO WWII SWABBIES.
    (THE U.S. NAVY MASCOT IS A GOAT.)

Letter To
Bishop Fiorenza

Donald J. Cole, October 25, 2004
Cypress, TX

Rt. Reverend Joseph Fiorenza, Bishop

Diocese of Galveston-Houston

1700 San Jacinto

Houston, TX 77002

Dear Bishop Fiorenza:

On Sunday, September 12, 2004, the "Social Justice" ministry of St. Anne's Parish, Tomball, Texas, conducted a voter registration drive after the Masses.

I am appalled and offended by the so-called "Social Justice" ministry's tainted conduct of the event. One of the women conducting the drive wore a tee shirt with an insulting and offensive message printed on it.

Emblazoned on the shirt was the statement: "Fair U. S. Elections . . . brought to you by the international monitors of Pax Christi International".

I asked the woman why she was wearing the shirt with the offending message. She informed me that it was part of a voter awareness drive sponsored by the USCCB and Pax Christi International.

265

The offensive message on that shirt insinuates that we Americans need an outside group to oversee U.S. elections to ensure fairness. Am I to believe that the USCCB is party to an offensive implication that elections are not fair in America? If that is the case I can only conclude that the failures of the American Bishops in recent years extend further than I was aware.

I will state, without fear of any credible contradiction, that America stands alone in the world of nations as the beacon of freedom for all other nations to follow, where free and fair elections are the only kind of elections we conduct. The Marxist, America hating, baseless blather of the left to the contrary, we neither need nor welcome any international monitors from the left wing Pax Christi or any other America hating organization to ensure free and fair elections.

As a lifelong, practicing Catholic soldier of Christ, I am deeply offended that Pax Christi, the so-called "Catholic" organization dares to demean the memory and the sacrifice of the millions of Americans who sacrificed their very lives to protect and preserve America's free and fair elections. I would be doubly offended to learn that the USCCB had a hand in such behavior. Please tell me it is not true.

If, in fact, it is true, Bishop, I would have to say that the Bishops and the USCCB would be better advised to use their leadership position to counsel Catholics not to scandalize themselves or the Church by voting for

266

"Counterfeit Catholic" politicians who run for high office, than to insinuate that we don't have fair elections.

By "Counterfeit Catholics" I refer, of course, to those politicians who, as if their earlier treasonous activities against our nation were not harmful enough, also scandalize Catholics, and our Church. Such arrogant, morally bankrupt politicians, while proclaiming themselves to the world to be Catholics, brazenly stand in defiance of Catholic doctrine and teaching, and even Papal authority.

These men and women flagrantly proclaim, support, endorse and advocate such issues as the culture of death of abortion, euthanasia, and other perversions, such as homosexual "marriage".

You know who these defenders of the culture of death, the promoters of perversion are. They are people like John Kerry, Nancy Pelosi, Tom Daschel, Teddy Kennedy, and numerous others of their ilk. I believe twenty-four of them signed a letter to the American Bishops, boldly warning the Bishops, in so many words, to "butt out". How utterly sad, to see.

The Bishops, who should be steadfast defenders of the Church, and leaders of the Faithful, have allowed (with a few courageous exceptions) such sinful behavior to go – not just unpunished – but unchallenged. How do faithful Catholics explain to our non-Catholic friends and neighbors (and our children as well) the failure of the Bishops to defend and lead our Holy Mother Church.

I have lived too long to expect much good to come from politicians of any stripe. But I still expect to see more than I do from our Bishops.

The scandals of recent years that have bedeviled our Church did not happen overnight, or in a vacuum. Bishop, you know that, I know that, and every thinking Catholic knows that. I see clear parallels between the moral decay reflected in the Church's scandals and the cancerous decline of morality in large parts of our national population. Those parallels lead back to the same approximate starting point in time – the mid-sixties when, in the wake of Vatican II, the wave of left wing permissiveness and perversion gave rise to the variety of destructive beliefs and behaviors that have taken such a huge toll upon the moral character of our people, both in and outside of the Church.

Though I am not one to submit to despair, I do not expect this little letter to have any substantial impact on you or the USCCB. In all candor, I honestly feel that my words here will fall upon deaf ears and that you will essentially turn a blind eye to this letter. But it was important to me and absolutely necessary that I write it.

There is another issue of great concern to me (and I know, to many, many others) that I must touch upon, vocations to the Priesthood. I will be as brief as I can.

Recently, several friends and I learned that seminarians at St. Mary's Seminary are required to pay for their own books. I was so stunned to hear that, I had difficulty believing it to be true. I have since been assured by numerous sources that it is indeed true. I have one question for you. Why? At a time when we so desperately need men in the priesthood, it is incomprehensible to me that those men would have to pay for anything related to their priestly formation. As a Knight of Columbus, it is my understanding that the seventy (70%) percent portion of the K of C State Charities assessment (from all of the accumulated Councils in the Diocese) that is returned annually to the Diocese, is used to contribute to the support of inner city Catholic Schools.

I would propose to you that a far better use for those funds would be to support all seminarians through their formation to ordination. My own K of C Council, like most Councils, currently contributes to the support of three seminarians. But that support is woefully short of the total needs.

I have absolute faith that Jesus will not allow his Church to fall – ever. But how troubling it is to see the wounds that have been inflicted on the American Church in the last forty odd years; wounds inflicted both from within the Church and from outside. And the Bishops have failed (again, with some notable exceptions) to restore the American Church. The enemies within the Church are the most despicable and, I believe, the most dangerous. I will simply say we need good priests in large numbers, and should be making heroic efforts to find them.

There is no disrespect to you or your Office intended in this letter. I respect you as a priest and Bishop and thank you for your fifty years of service to the Church. I know you are soon retiring, and will offer my prayers that you will enjoy many peaceful years of enjoyable and productive retirement.

Yours in Christ,

Donald J. Cole

Letter to the Editor, Tomball Potpourri

Donald J. Cole, October 31, 2000
Cypress, TX

To the Editor:

As a fifteen year veteran environmental professional and Certified Hazardous Materials Manager, I am rather astonished by Martin Marietta's plans to relocate their asphalt plant to a heavily populated part of "downtown Tomball" that is within spitting distance of many homes, several schools and churches. I do not reside in Tomball, but do attend church very near the proposed plant location.

My opposition to the plant is not a personal matter. It is based upon the negative impacts the plant would create for the people around it. I am even more astonished by the absence of any strong opposition to the proposed project by the Tomball City Council. Surely the proposed plant does not represent any significant potential tax windfall for the city. So why is the City Council amenable to allowing the plant in the midst of the homes and schools that would be negatively impacted by the plant?

Statements have been made claiming that the proposed plant's emissions of toxic materials – or potentially toxic materials – is far below allowable levels. Emission concentration levels are one factor in the evaluation process. Distance to potential receptors is a factor I believe to be even more important. The determination and assessment of emission levels that would be applied to the evaluation process are not based upon 100 percent, twenty-four hour, seven-day-per-week continuous monitoring of the plant.

Nor would the emissions be monitored 24/7 if a permit was issued and the plant was allowed to operate. The most fundamental truism regarding toxicity is that dose determines toxicity. Persons exposed to toxic – or potentially toxic- materials are subject to cumulative dose. The very young and the very old are particularly susceptible. No one can predict, with total accuracy, when one or more of the potential receptors (people) could or would accumulate a toxic dose of one or more of the potentially deadly constituents that will be released by the plant. People are too important to risk for an asphalt plant that can well be located elsewhere in a location that does not put people at risk.

I am not unsympathetic to Martin Marietta's or anyone else's wish to build an asphalt plant. But it should not be allowed at this particular location.

Donald J. Cole, - Tomball Area resident

Cole Sikes Letter

Donald J. Cole, January 7, 1999
Cypress, TX

Dear Cole,

Hi! I didn't get a chance to talk to you much on Christmas, what with the Turkey Frying and such.

But I want to tell you that the cutting board you made us for Christmas is really nice. You did a great job on it. You know I do a lot of the cooking around here, so you can be sure I will be using the cutting board a lot. I've bought many cutting boards over the years, all kinds of them. The best ones, by a mile, are wooden ones. And this wooden board you have made is the best one I've ever had. It is of very high quality.

In case you didn't know, and just so you will have this little piece of information to tuck away in your brain, wooden cutting/chopping boards are the best of all from a health standpoint. Studies have actually been conducted by scientific organizations to determine how many bacteria remain on cutting boards after they have been washed off and how long those bacteria remain active. The findings were that far fewer bacteria remain, after washing, on wooden boards than any other materials. Also, the bacteria that do remain after washing remain active for the shortest time on wooden boards – about fifteen minutes maximum, actually.

So, once again, thanks for the cutting board. It's a great present, even more so, since you made it with your own hands.

Good luck with your Soccer and your school work (the most important thing). Oh, one more thing I can't resist telling you. It's about the importance of the time you spend in school.

You probably never thought about it this way, but consider this: If you go all through elementary, junior high and high school, then go to college for four years to get your degree; then go to graduate school for another two years to get a masters' degree, you will have gone to school for what would appear to be eighteen years. Right? Well, yes and no.

You see, all through elementary, junior high and high school, you will spend about five and a half hours per day in classes. You only attend school about 180 days per year. If you multiply 180 (days) by 5.5 (hours per day) and multiply that total by 12 (total years for elementary, junior and senior high) you will get a total of 11, 880 hours. Then, if you multiply 5 (the average number of hours per day you will attend classes through college and graduate school) by 180 (the average number of days per year you will attend classes), and then multiply that total by 6 (the number of years for college and grad school) you will get a total of 5,400 hours. Now, if you add 5,400 and 11,880 together you will have a total of 17,280 hours.

There are twenty-four hours and three hundred and sixty-five days in a year. That's 8,760 hours. Doubling that for two years comes to 17,520 hours. So, you see, you will actually spend, in school, less than two years' total time. Putting it another way, you have only two years' time to prepare yourself for a lifetime that is expected today to last you just under eighty years. Need I say more?

O.K., I will leave you with this last bit of advice. If you should ever have to travel to an area of darkest Africa inhabited by cannibals, be sure to go there dressed as a service station attendant. Cannibals will not eat service station attendants. They give you gas, as we all know. Love, Grampa

Letter to The Editor, Houston Chronicle

Donald J. Cole, January 16, 1998
Cypress, TX

Dear Viewpoints Editor:

The Chronicle Editorial today: "Roe vs. Wade" states "The difference has become increasingly virulent". I agree.   Violence begets violence, and abortion is violence, that sets a horrible example.

The editorial goes on: "Women's lives depend on the ability to make reproductive choices safely and legally". Reproductive choices should be made before one creates a human life. In most cases the choice to abort has nothing to do with a woman's safety. It is a choice of convenience to the irresponsible, selfish person who makes it. It is simply a choice to kill, minus any requisite justification.

Again, quoting: "The message, of course, is that Roe was the right decision . . .". More than thirty million unborn human beings killed in the clinics since Roe are a bleak testimony to how horribly *wrong* Roe v. Wade was and is.

Shame on those who kill for convenience, and those who profit from the killing. Shame on us all, for not stopping the slaughter of the American Holocaust. More than thirty million and we are still counting.

Sincerely,

Donald J. Cole

Notes from the Author:

Commentary on the following Ford Motor Company Correspondence

As what I would characterize as a lifelong Ford Customer and booster of more than thirty years, I was astounded and extremely offended by the unpleasant and insulting experience I was subjected to by the company in the late nineties.

The letters that follow are self explanatory and offer a clear picture of the situation as it developed and played out. When My research revealed in early 1998 that I would not be allowed to bring suit against Ford for violating "Implied Warranty" (I learned at the time that Auto manufacturers were exempt in Texas from lawsuits over "Implied Warranty" – there's likely an interesting back-story there) I reconciled myself to the idea that I had lost the battle.

When I received the letter, later that year, that Ford was going to reimburse me for all out of pocket costs, I was feeling much better about the whole affair. Then, when they decided to renege on that promise, I realized I could then sue for breach of contract.

The entire ordeal was a sad commentary on the shabby state of Ford Motor Company Top Management of the times.

In the end, I did sue in Small Claims Court for the amount Ford had withheld from the total of my out of pocket costs ($585.66). Ford stalled until the day before the court date and then called to settle with me.

I accepted their settlement offer because I was so fed up with the whole thing. I am certain that, under the circumstances, I would have prevailed in court and would have been entitled to treble damages. But I have never been a greedy man and it meant more to me to show that I had more class than all of the top management jerks at Ford. As for whether or not I'll ever buy anything from Ford again, as much as I like their cars . . . not going to happen. I might buy a used Ford car or truck some day. But Ford will not see any of my money for it. It would have to have been already paid off by the original buyer . . . not with part of the funds from my purchase of it.

Letter: Alex Trotman Ford Motor Company

Donald J. Cole, December 30, 1997
Cypress, TX

Alex Trotman, President

Ford Motor Company

300 Renaissance Center

P.O. Box 43360

Detroit, MI 48243

Dear Mr. Trotman:

I found it annoying that I was required to provide my name and zip code before the telephone attendant on the Ford Customer Assistance line would give me your name and mailing address, as if I was asking for some sort of restricted information. It seems to me that the name and address of the President of Ford Motor Company should be freely available to anyone who asks for it, without having to first provide qualifying information.

I am writing to inform you of a grossly negative experience I have had with my 1995 Ford Windstar Van,

VIN: 2FM▮▮▮▮▮▮▮▮▮▮▮▮▮. I purchased the vehicle a little over four and a half months ago from the original owner (buyer). The vehicle had 33,800 miles on it when I bought it. I contacted Ford at that time to see if I could purchase an extended warranty on the van, since it still had less than 36,000 miles on it. I was informed that the extended warranty was not available to me. Since that time, I have had information that I should have at least been allowed to pay a fee of $100.00 or so to transfer the power train warranty. This option was not mentioned to me.

During the week of December 7, I was experiencing problems with my temperature gauge. The needle was literally bouncing up and down from bottom to top. I called a local dealer service department and described the problem. I was told the problem was probably a faulty sensor, or the gauge itself. I had to make an out of town trip that week and left the van at the airport on Wednesday, December 10, picking it up on my return late Friday night, December 12. On the drive home from the airport the temperature gauge seemed to be okay. On the next day, Saturday, December 13, the gauge was acting erratically again. I had checked several times to see if the engine was indeed heating up. It was not.

There was, however, a small loss of coolant. Twice during that week, I added about eight ounces of coolant to bring the level up to where it should be. I searched for the source of a leak, but could find none.

On Sunday evening, December 14, as my wife and I were returning home from a dinner engagement, the "check engine" light came on. We continued the additional four or five miles home and parked the van for the night. I know the check engine light indicates a problem with a computer function, so I planned to have it checked the next day. On Monday afternoon, when I prepared to leave home, the check engine light was still coming on. I checked the coolant and oil and topped them off – about eight ounces of coolant and a half-quart of oil. I left to go to my bank and then to the shop to have the van checked out. I drove about a mile, when the engine began to run rough and a large plume of steamy smoke was discharged from the tailpipe. I pulled over and parked the van immediately, called AAA and had the van towed to the Cillis Car Care Center shop, here in Cypress.

On Tuesday morning, December 16, Greg Cillis called me to confirm that there was a blown head gasket and probably a problem with one or more sensors, which he could not yet confirm because of the blown head gasket. Greg informed me that he had seen this problem before (blown head gasket on a low mileage engine) on this particular type Ford engine. He explained that Ford was aware that there was a

problem and advised me to call Ford before having him proceed with the repair. Greg felt sure that Ford would take care of the repair as warranty work due to the low mileage and the fact that it was a premature defect that has been seen before on the same type engine. It is quite rare in my experience to have an independent garage owner advise a customer to seek help from the manufacturer before having him do the work. But Cillis Car Care Center is a family owned local business well known for their quality work and, more importantly, their integrity.

I took Greg's advice and called two dealer service departments. I called Lone Star Ford, the dealership that originally sold the vehicle to Mr. Doan, from whom I bought the van in August, and spoke to Brad Stapp, the Service Manager. I explained the situation and details. Mr. Stapp's response was somewhere between curt and rude. He scoffed at the suggestion that this was a recurring problem with this particular engine type and said there was no such problem, period. He said they could do nothing for me. He said that if I were the original owner, it would be a different story. Next I called Marshall Ford in Hempstead, Texas and spoke with their Service Manager.

He was polite and explained that he did not personally know of such a problem, and that he didn't believe there was a "program" on it. He gave me the number for the Ford Customer Assistance Center.

I called the Customer Assistance Center and was informed that there was no "program" on the problem and Ford could do nothing about it. I was given information about a hood recall on my vehicle and

283

asked to provide my name, address, etc. as the new owner so I could receive any pertinent future notifications. No doubt my name will also be added to the list of Windstar owners that Ford will probably sell to others with something they want to pitch to me.

I have also learned, since buying the van from Mr. Doan, that the transmission on this vehicle was inspected, tested, diagnosed to be defective and overhauled at 28,164 miles. That work was done at Champion Ford in Houston between 07:18 December 13, 1996 and 18:00 December 16, 1996. I have the paperwork on the repair. I believe this is one of those vehicles that was not built, as it should have been back on April 14, 1994.

Now that I have provided you with all of the above details, I want to make you aware of the fact that I have been the owner of nothing but Ford vehicles since the early 1960's.

I have owned only Fords except for a Mercury Sable and a Merkur XR4TI we owned from 1986 to 1990. I still own a 1990 Ford Ranger that I bought in 1989. I have owned Galaxie 500's, Torinos, Mustangs Tauruses and others over the years.

It is inconceivable to me that Ford would want to save a few dollars by not accepting the responsibility for a repair that is clearly Ford's responsibility at the expense of losing a virtual lifetime Ford customer and booster (who has influenced many Ford vehicle purchases by family, friends and business associates).

My position is quite simple and uncomplicated. Because I was denied assistance by Ford, I had to pay Cillis Car Care Center $ 1,407.89 to repair my van. (A very fair price I might add) I would like you to instruct the appropriate departmental individual(s) to take quick action to reimburse me for the cost of the repair.

Please understand, Mr. Trotman, this not a "demand" letter. I am simply asking you to do the right thing. I am a sixty-two year old grandparent raising, together with my wife, two grandchildren, ages eleven and fifteen (soon to be sixteen and driving) and caring for my wife's aging mother. I am a self employed Environmental Consultant and Construction Manager, self employed because I have twice been a casualty of the prevailing corporate downsizing mania. I won't bore you with a litany of my problems. I am tough and resourceful. Being a "victim" is not in my makeup. I will add this. With the load I am carrying, I can't afford to lose $ 1,407.89.

I will reiterate: this is not a "demand". However, please be aware that I need relief. I trust that Ford would want to do the right thing and not make a mortal enemy or an Anti-Ford activist out of a long time loyal customer and booster. I can think of at least a few other legal remedies I could, and would be forced to, pursue if Ford were to deny my simple request, any of which would certainly be more costly to Ford than granting my request for prompt reimbursement of my out of pocket loss.

I am enclosing copies of the paperwork for both the repairs I had to have done, and the previous work on the transmission. I would be glad to answer any questions you may have and I will hold to my belief that you will choose to make things right and preserve the good relationship I have had with Ford for all these many years. I look forward to hearing from you or whomever you designate to handle this matter soon. With Best Wishes for continued success in the New Year, I am

Sincerely,

Donald J. Cole

Letter: General Counsel Ford Motor Company

Donald J. Cole, January 14, 1998
Cypress, TX

Ford Motor Company

Office of the General Counsel

Park Lane Towers West, Suite 400

Three Park Lane Boulevard

Dearborn, MI 48126

Dear Counsel:

On December 30, 1997, I wrote to Mr. Alex Trotman concerning a problem I had with my Ford Windstar van. I requested that Mr. Trotman take action to reimburse me for the costs I incurred for the repair of my van. You can get further details by referring to my letter of December 30, and its attachments,

Today I received a telephone call from Mr. Christian Ruttgers a Ford Customer Service Representative. Mr. Ruttgers informed me that my letter to Mr. Trotman was passed down to him to handle. He also informed me that the department in which he works handles all mail directed to Mr. Trotman, and that Mr. Trotman had not, himself, seen my letter. I shall resist the urge to comment on the quality of Ford's customer service, beyond saying that my telephone conversation with Mr. Ruttgers had me flashing back on a book I read years ago, entitled "The Suicidal Corporation". The book should be a must read for Ford executives and employees.

Mr. Ruttgers informed me that Ford Motor Company would not do anything for me to cover the costs of the repairs of the premature defects in my vehicle. I asked Mr. Ruttgers for the name of his direct supervisor. After resisting my request for a time, he gave me the name of Nancy Vert, whom he claimed is his supervisor. I told him I wished to speak with her and asked him to connect me with her line. Mr. Ruttgers refused to do so. I asked to be connected to the corporate legal department and was told he did not know the number. He did give me the address to which this letter is directed. Another request to speak with Ms. Vert was also refused by Mr. Ruttgers. Also, Mr. Ruttgers said he could not provide me with the name and address of Ford's Agent for Service in Texas and could not connect me to the legal department or anyone who could provide me with that information.

The purpose of this letter is to inform you that I am very disappointed by the manner in which Ford has handled this situation. Mr. Ruttgers told me he was instructed to "do the right thing" about my letter. I asked him what his definition was of "the right thing". He made no response. I told him my definition of "the right thing" was for Ford to reimburse me for my out of pocket costs for the repairs of the premature defect. I am frankly surprised that a reasoned letter to a top corporate executive would be handled so poorly. I am equally surprised that Ford is so willing to lose a long time (over thirty years) loyal customer whose influence and opinion has resulted in the purchase of many ford products by other people who have asked for my advice over the years.

Finally, Mr. Ruttgers made references to my future dealings with Ford. That's an oxymoron. I explained to Mr. Ruttgers that there is no "future" between me and Ford if this is the best Ford can do. It is unfortunate for both sides that Ford has apparently, and illogically, chosen to make an enemy of a friend.   I am one individual who will not voluntarily be anyone's victim. Please be advised that I intend seek relief from the courts. Despite Mr. Ruttgers' uncooperative responses I have secured, from the Texas Secretary of State's office, the name and address of CT Corporation System, Ford's Registered Agent in Texas.

This is my formal notice to you that unless Ford Motor Company reverses its present position and makes me an acceptable offer in settlement of this matter within ten days from the date of receipt of this letter, I will conclude that Ford does not wish to settle the matter amicably, and preserve the good will of a long time customer.

Failing to receive a favorable response with the ten-day period, I shall have Ford's Registered Agent in Texas served with legal process and let the matter be decided in the courts. I would prefer an amicable solution. The choice is Ford's to make. Should you wish to discuss the matter, I can be reached, at: 281- 37X-XXXX (telephone), or 281-37X-XXXX (fax).

Sincerely,

Donald J. Cole

Letter:
Vehicle Service and
Programs
Ford Motor Company

Donald J. Cole, July 13, 1998
Cypress, TX

A.R. Kaduk, Manager

Vehicle Service and Programs

Ford Motor Company, Customer Service Division

P.O. Box 1904

Dearborn, MI 48121-1904

RE: Service Program Number 98M01

   1995 Ford Windstar, VIN
2FM ██████████████

Dear Mr. or Ms. Kaduk:

Recently, I received a telephone call from a person from Ford's "Customer Satisfaction" department, thanking me for having written to Ford concerning my Windstar. The person told me he thought he would be able to get me reimbursed for the repairs I had to have done on the Windstar. I was instructed to bring the original receipt for the work to a local Ford dealership. I did that. I brought the receipt to Tomball Ford and turned it over to the service manager, Rick Boen. About a week later, I received a check from Tomball Ford for $822.23.

Since I had exhausted all avenues I had open to me to recover my out of pocket costs for the repair to the Windstar caused by the premature failure of the engine head gaskets I was surprised at the turn of events that led to the re-imbursement.

I had written to top management, Alex Trotman and the Office of the General Counsel asking for reimbursement, to no avail. I notified Ford in subsequent letters that I would file suit to recover my loss, only to learn through my own research that I would not be able to make a case under the doctrine of "implied warranty". Upon discovering that, I abandoned my plans to sue. I decided that I would simply accept Ford's decision to make an enemy of me, though I had been a loyal Ford customer and booster for more than thirty years.

++I determined that I would never buy another Ford product *from Ford or any Ford Dealer*, and would use my influence with other people to convince them *to not buy Ford because Ford was not worthy of their trust.*

It is an interesting conundrum. You see, I believe Ford builds excellent cars and trucks. But every manufacturer builds an occasional lemon or a vehicle with defects that shouldn't be there. When that happens, the customer relies on the integrity of the Manufacturer and its representatives to make things right for the customer. That is precisely what Ford steadfastly refused to do for me.

Let me bring you up to date on what has transpired since April, 1998, when I discovered I could not bring a successful lawsuit against Ford, under "implied warranty", for the premature defects in my Windstar and the damage that resulted from the defect.

In May, 1998, I bought a 1992 Ford Tempo for my Granddaughter who just got her driver's license. Of course I bought the car from an individual, not from a Ford dealer. Ford won't see any money from the purchase. I decided to sell the Windstar

as soon as possible and replace it with another vehicle. I had new brakes put on and had the van detailed. I sold the Windstar. I also sold my 1990 Ford Ranger – probably the most reliable, trouble free vehicle I've ever owned. I have bought two new vehicles, a 1998 Jeep Grand Cherokee and a

1998 Cadillac Catera. I've enclosed copies of photos of the two new vehicles. The Jeep would have been a Ford Explorer. The Cadillac would have been a Mercury or Lincoln, had Ford not made it clear to me that I was not a valued customer.

Will I ever buy another Ford product? I really don't know. There would have to be some compelling reason that I cannot envision at this point in time. As to the other part of my plan to respond to the shabby treatment I received from Ford; my plan to use my influence to convince others not to buy from Ford, I will let that go. Of course, I will not be making any efforts to convince anyone to buy either.

Now let me get to the main point of this letter. Two weeks ago, I received your letter, dated June, 1998 and postmarked (metered) Southgate, MI, June 25, 1998. Your letter references the above captioned Service Program and related information. I call your attention to the section "Refunds" at the top of page two, which informs me:

"If you paid to have this service performed prior to the date of this letter, Ford is offering a full refund." As we both know, I did pay to have the work done before the date of your letter. I paid $1,407.89 to repair the damage caused by the defective head gaskets (copy of receipt attached – original given to Tomball Ford at your request). The check I received from Tomball Ford was for $822.23. That is $585.66 short of the "full refund" you have promised in your letter.

I called Rick Boen at Tomball Ford to ask what the $822.23 figure was comprised of. He informed me that the amount reflected the cost of replacing the head gaskets but not for the valve job, which he claimed was not necessary. His statement is patently incorrect. **All of the work that was done was necessary**. When the head gaskets failed, there were valves burned and sensors sustained damage as well.

Your letter promises a "full refund" for repairs that were necessary as a result of a premature defective condition you have acknowledged that resulted in failure of the head gaskets on my Windstar, in turn, resulting in all of the damage that I had repaired by a local shop well known for its impeccable integrity. I reject Mr. Boen's claim that the excluded costs were for work that was not necessary. I believe any jury in the land would also. We are not dealing now with a case of "implied warranty". Rather, this is a case of the promise of a "full refund" for work done to repair damage caused by an acknowledged defect.

By acknowledging the defect and instituting the program Ford has taken a step in the right direction. Surely, you do not now wish to take two steps backward by refusing to honor your pledge of a full refund to an already aggrieved customer.

Please consider this letter my formal request for reimbursement of the $585.66 that was improperly withheld. I will send this letter via certified mail. If the remaining $585.66 due me is not received within ten days of your receipt of this letter, please be assured that I will file suit to recover the withheld amount plus all costs incurred since the engine failure in December, 1997 and punitive damages. I trust reason and good sense will prevail. Thank you for your attention to this important matter.

Sincerely, Donald J. Cole

Letter to The Editor, Houston Chronicle

Donald J. Cole, November 1, 1996
Cypress, TX

Dear Viewpoints Editor:

The Chronicle does its readers a disservice with its series of Editorials, "Ballpark I-IV". Here's my response. I hope you put aside your bias and print it. You state in Ballpark II that building the Astrodome (*Harris County Domed Stadium*) has "given Houston a reputation for innovation and Houstonians (*Harris Countians, actually*) the image of being doers" (*parenthetic remarks, mine*). We are, indeed, innovative doers. That simple fact is precisely why we Harris Countians should firmly reject Proposition 1 – "The Ballpark Heist". Since when is it good counsel to pay a blackmailer?

Harris County should show the nation once again that we are innovators and doers by showing at the polls we don't roll over for blackmailers, especially poor little rich boy blackmailers. The oilers are gone. Good Riddance. They and their owner have been losers for years. Now, poor Drayton (He thought the Dome was fine, less than a year ago) says if we don't build him a new playpen, he'll take his ball and go home. Go for it, Mac. Let's see if your Virginia connection really can – and will – buy your chokers. This is Harris County. We'll survive. More. We will continue to thrive. Maybe we will buy another team and move them here; create a new league. Heck, maybe we will create a whole new sport to replace football and baseball. The possibilities are limitless. Those who think we will wither up and blow away if we don't have an NFL or National League team, are suffering from a serious case of what I call Recto-Cranial Inversion.

Tonight, I saw George Bush on TV, pitching for Prop 1. (I can't stop shaking my head) I always admired and respected Mr. Bush. I worked for his 1970 Senate campaign. I supported him in all of his elections since then, including the 1992 presidential campaign; was at the rally the night before the election. It's funny, though, tonight all I could think of, watching his pitch, was "Read my lips . . .". Sorry, Mr. President, I still admire and respect you, but you lost me on this one. I'd like to see baseball and football remain in Houston, but not on the terms of Prop 1. As for the Rodeo, let them get the scalpers to pony up some bucks. It seems only fair. After all, they sell all the tickets to the scalpers, don't they?

We're still paying off the last grand refurbishment of the Dome. I'm voting NO on Prop 1 and urge all my Harris County Neighbors to do the same.

I hope they get to read this letter. I reckon that's up to you, Ms. Editor.

Letter to The Editor, Houston Chronicle

Cypress, TX January 24, 1995

Dear Editor:

The tumultuous events we have seen in recent times at abortions "clinics" point to one simple truth: Abortion cheapens human life. The so-called pro-choice activists point to the killings of abortionists and their assistants and claim they are the result of the activities of Pro-Life demonstrators. That claim is a lie. The murders of the abortionists and their assistants are the direct result of the systematic killing of unborn human beings which they practice in their so-called clinics.

When the indiscriminate killing of unborn children stops, the murders of abortionists also will stop. The term "Pro-Choice", as it relates to the abortion issue, really means "Pro-Abortion". In turn, "Pro-Abortion" means "Pro-Killing".

Pro-Life proponents, including both demonstrators and non-demonstrators alike, have only one goal – to respect and preserve life. It is sad and unfortunate that there are unstable people among us who carry out horrible acts of violence like the murders at the so-called "clinics". These individuals were not encouraged by those who are Pro-Life. They followed the example set by their victims; were motivated to violence as a result of the violence practiced by their victims, day after day at those "clinics of death".

More than thirty million unborn children have been slaughtered at those "clinics" since the "Roe vs Wade" decision two decades ago. Thirty million! How tragic we have become as a nation. That the American people have stood by for so long and allowed this modern "holocaust" to continue is a stinging indictment of our loss of National Character. Shame on those who do the killing, on both sides of the issue. Shame on those who point the finger of blame at those who would preserve life. Shame on those who profit from the killing. Shame on us all for not stopping the slaughter. God bless America . . .For What?

Sincerely,

Donald J. Cole

Letter to Senator Bob Livingston

Donald J. Cole, January 24, 1994
Kenner, LA

Honorable Bob Livingston

U. S. House Of Representatives

Washington, DC 20515

Dear Congressman Livingston:

I am writing to inform you of my concerns about the proposed so called Health Care Reform Package. My concerns are twofold.

First. While I believe that there is a genuine need for improvement in the health care system relative to ensuring that decent health care is made available to all Americans, I do not believe socialized medicine is the way to accomplish improvement. To the contrary, I believe that the proposed system would do more to hurt than it would do to help. I am outraged that our government is attempting to inflict a discredited, failed everywhere Socialist system on those of us who make the country work. What we need is for the government to get out of the way of quality health care for all Americans.

A voucher system coupled with a genuine program to rid the system of the rampant fraud would give us what we need. Like most people I know, I want a qualified Physician prescribing for me, not a bureaucrat or an unmotivated civil service leech.

Second. I am further outraged by the fact that this alleged Health Care Package includes taxpayer funded payment for abortion on demand. That, Sir, would be an abridgement of my freedom of religion, since my religious beliefs preclude my support of abortion. Abortion is not health care. Abortion kills a life. My opposition to abortion is not founded on religious grounds alone. By using federal funds, money taken from the taxpayers, the government is also a participant in the killing. This government has no such right, no legitimate power to kill its defenseless unborn. The Supreme Court's infamous Roe v. Wade decision twenty one years ago set this nation on a disgraceful course which has resulted in a modern holocaust that is unparalleled in history - more than thirty million innocent lives. Shame on us all, for allowing the slaughter to continue.

I ask that you cast your vote to send the so called Health Care Package back to the drawing board and I urge you to vote against inclusion of abortion on demand in any Health Care Package. I would like to have your written response, sir, on these troubling issues.

Sincerely,

Donald J. Cole

Letter to The Editor, Houston Post

Donald J. Cole, September 1, 1992
Houston, TX

Dear Sound-Off Editor:

Maybe I dozed off, missed the commentary on radio and TV, didn't get my copy of The Houston Post that morning.

Whatever, I have yet to hear or read any reaction to the best speech delivered to the Republican National Convention. I refer to Labor Secretary Lynn Martin's dynamic nominating speech.

"You can't be one kind of man and another kind of President", she said. Several times, she repeated the words with conviction. She made the point!

She stunned everyone in the Astrodome, and the viewing audience when she had the "stuff" to ask, "Are you better off today than you were four years ago?".

She answered the question for us. "Of course you are", she declared, and went on to list the reasons: The fall of Communism; the disintegration of the Soviet Union; the destruction of the Berlin Wall; the comfort of sleeping without the threat of nuclear war hovering over us. Great speech! I only wish that Secretary Martin had completed – the rest of the story.

Tremendous accomplishments, those above, won for a price. Now we must show our "*Our* Stuff", accept the price of victory and get on to the next battle. Kick out the good-for-nothing Democrat Congress and give President Bush the support he needs to win the battle of the economy.

Sincerely,

Donald J. Cole

Letter to The Editor, The Houston Post

Donald J. Cole, January 29, 1992
Houston, TX

Here we go again! The Japs are at it again. It must be a fifty-year cycle.

In 1941, the Japs set out to prove something to the world. The historical record documents that they did prove, conclusively, their monumental stupidity. For decades, the Japan, Inc. War Lords built their war machine, bullied their neighbors, and then convinced themselves that they could conquer the greatest nation this earth has ever seen, or ever will see.

There's a different spin on it this time around.

The last few decades, since the American taxpayer rebuilt their country, have seen the Japs stealing all of the technology they have, using their captive workforce and their corrupt Government/Industry complex to steal markets from us the world over and generally biting the hands that fed and nurtured them back to health.

Apparently, once again, these weird people have convinced themselves they can conquer the United

305

States of America. This time, it's economic warfare. Amazing! The stupidity of the Japs must be a genetic thing.

Japan will never conquer this Nation, by military, or economic, or any means. Their pathetic closed, vertical society will never achieve real greatness at anything. They simply don't have what it takes. They never will.

We have many problems in our country, by-products of our diversity. In the end, though, the multitude and diversity of our ethnic and racial threads combine to make the fabric of America indestructible. The Japs and others like them will never understand our greatness, and will continue to underestimate the fundamental, common will that will always see us through difficult times.

Take heart, folks. The time is fast approaching for us to give the Japs another richly deserved whipping. This time it won't require bombs and bloodshed.

Letter to The Editor, Houston Post

Donald J. Cole, Summer, 1991
Houston, TX

Dear Sound-Off Editor:

What's wrong with America can be summed up in three words: the American People. We blame everyone from the President to the drug addicts for what ails us, but we do not act.

We can fix America.

Register to vote. Study the issues. Vote as intelligently as we can. Work for positive change – some examples:"

Limit terms of House members to one six-year term; Pass a balanced Budget Amendment; Give the President line item veto power; Enact a flat-rate income tax; Abolish the IRS; Abolish the capital gains tax; Phase out Social Security and replace it with a mandatory private sector IRA program; Provide Welfare to the aged and infirm, taxable "Workfare" to the able-bodied; Abolish Plea-Bargaining; Lock up the criminals; Eliminate all quota systems and "so-called"

Minority, Affirmative Action or Disadvantaged programs; Stop the American Genocide of Abortion as contraception and genetic selection; Enact a mandatory, two-year public service obligation, civilian or military, for all young Americans; Pass a voting Responsibility Amendment, requiring all "eligible" Americans to vote or be severely penalized.

Will we meet the challenge? Then first, register to vote. Consider voluntarily assuming personal responsibility to get another person to register; maybe two, three, or twenty.

Sincerely,

Donald J. Cole

REFLECTIONS . . .

Fujiyama

Donald J. Cole, 2000
Cypress, TX

It was rapidly approaching that melancholy hour of the day when afternoon transforms itself into evening, like the flame of a warming fire dwindling into a glow of embers.

Fujiyama, its graceful crown white with snow, was boldly silhouetted against the persimmon sky. "How odd", I thought, "that my first glimpse of the Land of the Rising Sun should be at sunset". Even more unusual, in retrospect, is that I have no recollection of the sun's rising ever in the many months I spent in Japan. In stark contrast, my memory abounds with pictures of sunsets of startling dimensions.

A ship, as any man who has sailed the seas will attest, has a distinct personality. On that crisp September evening, those many years ago, the ship, the aircraft carrier USS Yorktown, seemed to be as captivated as we crewmen were by the breathtaking beauty of the spectacle before her. She seemed quieter, rode more smoothly through the waters of the Sea of Japan, as if trying not to disturb the scene. Absurd? Perhaps, yet the sensation was there nonetheless.

By the time all lines were secured and the gangway was hoisted aboard at Piedmont Pier, darkness had fallen and a chill wind had come down from the north-northwest.

Piedmont Pier, Yokosuka, Japan! Piedmont Pier, its huge motor crane towering alongside Yorktown, rose many stories above us. The realization that here, from this very shipyard, the Japanese had launched hundreds of warships less than ten years previously in their shameful, failed attempt to become a dominating world power. Indeed, one of those ships, Japan's mightiest battleship, the Yamato, had been sunk . . . sent to the bottom of the sea by the bombs from the planes of our own USS Yorktown. It was almost too much for my mind to process.

"Slowly", I remember thinking. "Take it in slowly, a little at a time. What will they be like . . . these Japs", I wondered. "Probably ugly, sinister, repulsive little creatures", I thought in silence.

The John Q. Public Press Release That Never Was And Its Aftermath

Donald J. Cole, October 2, 1984
San Francisco, CA

"D. J. Cole and L.S. Jones have scheduled a Press Conference at 3:00 P.M. today to announce the formation of a Limited Partnership, Known as "JOHN Q. PUBLIC, LTD.".

The Partnership is being formed to raise fifty million dollars ($50,000.000.00) to purchase the San Francisco Giants Baseball Team.

Cole said partnerships in the new company will be offered to the general public in two thousand dollar ($2,000.00) increments. Jones added that once the

purchase of The Giants is complete, the partnership will look into the possibility of converting Candlestick Park into a domed facility.

Cole, of Anaheim Hills, CA and Jones, of Raceland, LA, both engineers with the Oil & Gas Division of John

Brown Engineers & Constructors, Inc. said they plan to keep the team in San Francisco.

Today's Press Conference will be held at 3:00 P.M. at the foot of Market Street."

****

I wrote The Faux Press Conference Announcement above as an inside joke for the John Brown Engineers & Construction, Inc. Team that was on temporary assignment at the Beale Street, San Francisco Headquarters of Bechtel Corporation, conducting a Quality and Constructability Review for an Offshore Oil platform Project that was to be built for an Offshore California location in Federal Waters.

Bechtel Corporation was the Engineering Contractor for the Project. John Brown Engineers & Constructors, Inc. was the Construction Management Contractor for the Project. The review was very detailed, tedious, and demanding on the members of the JBE&C team.

Coincidently, during the period the review was going on, San Francisco Giants Team Owner Bob Lurie, was wringing his hands over the financial losses he was sustaining, and his frustration with the weather conditions at Candlestick Park. It was playing all over the local media and came across to most members of the JBE&C team, most of them from Texas and Louisiana as a silly Soap Opera. Lurie, himself, seemed to most of the team to be something of a sad sack cry

313

baby. (See "Lurie For Selling Giants San Francisco, Oct.1 (UPI))

As the team member responsible for housing and transportation arrangements and bi-weekly weekend rotations, I was always watching stress accumulations, which had a direct relationship to productivity levels.

Thus, I hatched the idea of the Faux Press Release to give the JBE&C Review Team a few laughs and relieve a bit of stress. I drafted the announcement, typed it up and distributed it around among the team, within the area of the building that we occupied. It had the desired effect. Everyone had a laugh and it reduced the stress level for the guys.

But it didn't end there . . .

A few weeks later, I was part of a group of our team members and several of JBE&C's Oil & Gas Division management people from Houston Headquarters. This group made a trip to Ensenada, Mexico to evaluate a proposed site for a shipyard. The owners of the proposed yard wanted to be considered for the contract to build the Platform. The Site Evaluation team traveled to San Diego and checked into one of the major hotels on Shelter Island to spend the night before the drive down to Ensenada.

It happened that the L. A. Dodgers were in town to play the San Diego padres the next day. The JBE&C team, relaxing in the lobby Lounge for a drink before dinner noted the presence of several Dodger players in the Lounge.

Then it happened . . . The Dodger players were seated close by and their conversation could be heard clearly.

The JBE&C guys had all but forgotten the amusing Imaginary Press Conference of several days before. But one of the guys couldn't believe his ears, when he directed our attention to the subject of the Dodgers conversation: the **"BIG RUMOR" . . .** that there was some kind of citizens group forming in San Francisco to buy the San Francisco Giants!

Sam Jones and I, reflecting on the caper a couple of years later, lamented the fact that we did not actually go through with the "Press Conference" and see what happened.

No one will ever know.

To A wife, Sleeping (Two)

Donald J. Cole, January 28, 1968
Houston, TX

The love I have for you is not a fleeting thing as poets have said. To the contrary, it is as constant as time itself, always there; never stopping. It is not any longer a youthful love; nor is it a "story-book" love, all decked out in hearts and flowers. Indeed, sometimes in this sad world, it is not even a happy love. It is, however, always a true love.

My love is not put on display like a fourth of July fireworks display. It is rather, more like a rainbow – always there, but seen only at certain times. And doesn't a rainbow appear more beautiful . . . because it is not a frequent sight?

Just as my love for you is not always a happy thing it is, also, occasionally a painful thing – for you, or for me, or both of us. None of this, however, serves to diminish my love for you. It will live in me in constant intensity for as long as I draw breath on this earth.

I Love You.

To A Wife, Sleeping (One)

Donald J. Cole,   October 12, 1967
Houston, TX

Arriving home to find you sleeping, I wonder where
your dreams have taken you. I watch you . . . quietly.
You look younger in sleep. Your face not burdened by
the worries of the day's routine, your brow without a
crease, you fairly *glow*!

The pillow plays rude tricks on your hair, yet your real
beauty doesn't rely on pretty hairdos or other such
contrivances. Your real beauty needs nothing to adorn
it, for it is felt, rather than seen, radiated from within
you.

Thinking these thoughts, I ponder my great fortune.
How lucky I am that you are *my wife* and not someone
else's.

ABOUT THE AUTHOR:

Military, Education, Bureaucracy, Trade and more . . . anchored by a call to abolish the Party System that the Founders warned against and wanted no part of. Today, we see before us the result the Founders envisioned. The Parties are who and what are responsible for the destruction that has been inflicted upon our embattled Republic. We must get the Nation back on the right track. **Help Us Get Job Done!**

A second generation American, born into an American-Irish, Catholic family near the end of the great depression, the second of four children, Mr. Cole's deep sense of patriotism was born in him as a young boy growing up in Brooklyn, NY in the war years of the second world war. Even as an eight-year-old, his mind was occupied with matters of duty and patriotism and his prayers for his uncles and cousins who were in battle far off in Europe and the Pacific.

The Democrat politics embraced by all of his elders, though, never reached him. In the early days of his nearly fifty-seven year marriage to his beloved wife, Patsy, the two were "The Republicans" in their Brooklyn District. Six years later, they returned to Patsy's native Texas, and found themselves "The other Republicans" in heavily Democrat Corpus Christi.

Today, with more than fifty years of commitment and service to the Republican Party and the Conservative cause, he has come to understand a painful, but true, reality. Although the Texas Republican Party has grown tremendously, the GOP has become so much like the Democrats that they are too much alike to tell them apart. Yet, the two Parties are terminally polarized by their self interests.

Conservatism and Patriotism have been savaged over the past five decades by both of the *Failed Parties*. In 2008, Mr. Cole made the decision to establish a grass-roots advocacy organization to promote and support across-the-board reform in America to end the slide and restore America's luster. The Organization, "No Parties America. Org" is committed to a range of reforms, including: Election & Campaign Reform, Reform of Judicial, Immigration, Tax,

Join Today! "NoPartiesAmerica.Org"